From Queens To
QUEENS:

*How the Madison
Drag Community Saved My Life*

by
Jaimie Sherling

From Queens To QUEENS:
How the Madison Drag Community Saved My Life

PUBLISHED BY: GWN Publishing | www.GWNPublishing.com

COVER DESIGN: Kristina Conatser – GFAD Design / LongBar Creative Solutions | www.longbarcreatives.com

ISBN: ISBN: 978-1-7367932-5-1

This book is dedicated to my FIVE family and
my most loved and fairest wife, whom
I love you so much.

CONTENTS

KNOW YOUR WORTH

PRETTY

MY OYSTER

I was born into royalty. Fine, you got me. If we're being technical, I was born in Queens, New York. Okay, the hospital was in Brooklyn.

My mom gave birth to me in the fall of 1976. I lived the first seven years of my life in Maspeth—a neighborhood in Queens. Then my dad's job transferred him, my mom, and all seven of us children to Florida. "You can take the girl out of the city . . ." You know that saying? I swear it was written about me. After four humid years, we moved back to upstate New York. Goodbye neighborhood pool and birthday parties at the beach.

Fast forward to the summer of 2001. Blissful in the warm, midday sun, I'd drifted off to sleep on the deck of my house in Madison, Wisconsin, when the phone rang. One look at the screen, and I had to answer. I hadn't heard from Lauren from my college dance group in ages. I tapped the screen. "Hey! What's up?"

"Ohmygodohmygodohmygod!" Lauren shrieked into my ear.

What was she freaking out about? It sounded like excitement, but perhaps there'd been a catastrophe. With her, you couldn't be sure.

"I'm going to be in a Broadway show!" Lauren exclaimed.

My jaw dropped. "Oh my god. That's amazing. Congratulations!" Knowing how hard she'd worked and for how many years, I brimmed over with pride. She'd earned the accomplishment. And I needed to see her on stage.

Plans came together quickly, and I looked forward to seeing her in a few months. I bounced around my house crossing days off the calendar like a kid counting down to Christmas morning.

Exactly a month before my departure, I started a typical day in my kindergarten classroom. I'd taught two years in California, and this was my first year in this school district. I quickly felt at home with my students and their families, enjoying the privilege of being their first "official" teacher. Minutes after our morning circle time, the teacher who taught next door peeked her head into the room. "Can you come here please?"

Assuming she needed an emergency bathroom break, I ran rather than walked into the storage closet between our classrooms.

"Someone flew a plane into the World Trade Center," she whispered.

What? I struggled to hold back sobs. Our principal didn't want us to share the news with our kindergarten classes. Somehow, I managed to teach the rest of the day without breaking down. For days afterward, I was in shock, then numb. But I figured Broadway didn't shut down, so neither could I.

Four weeks later, Lauren called again. "So, I won't be in the show this weekend."

Cue the sound of a record scratch. Had she gotten the flu? Broken her leg? And not in the good-luck theatrical kind of way. My brain raced through possibilities, but no words came out of my mouth.

"They needed me in the touring cast. I'm on my way to Florida."

What about what I needed? I was flying halfway across the country to see her on Broadway. I needed her to be in New York. I composed myself enough to tell her I understood. I would still go and have a great time in the city.

The next morning, I drove to the airport. Parking the car, I willed myself to calm down. I was nervous, naturally. After 9-11, was it really safe to fly? I told myself it was and got out of my car, tearing up as I walked through brand-new security protocols. Life was never going to be the way it was. Once I finally got onto the plane, I buckled myself into my seat and felt my shoulders relax a bit.

When I stepped outside LaGuardia airport, I exhaled deeply, more deeply than I had in a very long time. While the world around me spun in chaos, I had an immediate sense of relief. I was home.

The city was somber, and rubble still burned in lower Manhattan. Yet I knew I was exactly where I was supposed to be. While walking around, I noticed a billboard that read, "To people from all over the country who want to help: come here and spend money, go to a restaurant, see a show. The life of the city goes on."

Happy to be of service, I strolled into Rockefeller Center with a specific mission in mind. I found the elevator and pressed sixty-five. Butterflies fluttered around my stomach as the numbers climbed. One of the best views in the city, I treated myself to a cocktail in the famous Rainbow Room. It was as delicious as it was expensive.

Later on that weekend, I took in two Broadway shows. The spotlight shone on the costumes for *The Lion King*, and my heart jumped to my throat during the stampede. I sniveled because yes, yes, I could feel the love that Saturday night.

I didn't know it at the time, but the billboard that had welcomed me to the city would become a mantra for me. The life of the city goes on. At least I wanted it to.

Six months later, my mom called and derailed those plans. "Jaimie, the cancer is back." My throat went dry. I slumped onto the kitchen floor. Not again.

When I was a junior in high school, my dad was diagnosed with non-Hodgkin's lymphoma. Back then, as a self-absorbed teenager, I didn't closely follow his treatment. I only knew that he and my mom drove to Strong Memorial in Rochester a lot that year. And that he survived. Would we be that fortunate again? I was so worried. And felt so helpless. I lived halfway across the country from him. "What can I do, Mom?"

Knowing I didn't have much vacation time, she said, "Please pray for him."

And I did. Thanks to a stem cell transplant, he survived a second time. And I knew exactly how we'd celebrate.

Back in the days of Broadway Joe, my dad was a season ticket holder for the Jets. We decided to meet in the city, and I treated him to a game. We breathed in the mild October air, stadium hot dogs, and beer and joined in when the firefighter chanted, "J-E-T-S. Jets! Jets! Jets!"

Life goes on.

The following year, I was finally ready to be a mom. The plan was to return to my classroom after maternity leave. In the spring of 2004, I looked down at my growing belly. I was due in November. I thought about starting the school year nine months pregnant. Then I pictured my water breaking the first day of school and decided to stay home to raise my daughter.

At her first birthday party, I announced I was pregnant again. I definitely wasn't heading back to the classroom now. Over the next few years, my sleep-deprived fog morphed into managed chaos. But I wished for some time to myself. When my kids were seven and nine, I decided to get away for a bit. Mama needed a break.

New York City had been calling to me for years through my college friend Jen, who embodied the spirit of fun and joy. We'd had some great times together, including singing back-up in a band. She'd moved to New York, and I'd spent years following her adventures there. Naturally, I booked a flight to visit her.

The weekend I spent there remains one of the best weekends of my life. Days before the trip, Jen asked me what I wanted to do. Easy. I wanted to soak up the city and act as if I lived there.

"The world is your oyster!" she said, full of ideas as she picked me up from the airport. "You'll love the eighties show. It's at 11:30 pm, so if we need a nap in advance, that's cool. But otherwise, it's really about what you love. I can take you shopping for fab cheap clothes or fab pricey clothes. We can buy the world's best chocolate chip cookie. We can wander around the West Village. There's boozy brunch or delicious brunch. And twenty-dollar mani-pedis." Her hands punctuated the excitement in her voice. "We can go to the most amazing bath products store, walk in Central Park, paint pottery, get glitter tattoos, and visit a shockingly accurate psychic. We can eat self-serve FroYo. There are sixteen yogurt choices. We can walk 5th Ave, see a Broadway show, take a dance class, go to Magnolia Bakery, get new shoes, get a headpiece made for you in Soho." She finally stopped to take a breath. "Girl, in short, we can do anything." And those were my options for Saturday.

For the record, she did take me to get the world's best chocolate chip cookie. We walked from Central Park to Levain Bakery's original location. The smell of chocolate wafted onto the sidewalk while we waited. I was in love. The cookie was perfect. Slightly crunchy on the outside. Warm and gooey on the inside.

As I boarded the plane at the end of the weekend, my cheeks felt wet. I didn't want to go home to Madison. New York City was my home. At least it felt that way. And I made a promise to myself that I would go back more often. For me. For my heart.

Because life goes on.

Funny that on a trip years later, Jen mentioned, "You always seem to visit the city during pivotal points in your life." But we'll get to that later.

GO!

Have you ever made what you thought was a small decision that you later realized completely changed the course of your life? I haven't either. I'm so lying.

While I'd always loved musical theater, I never thought of auditioning for a show. Sure, I could carry a tune in a bucket. But me on stage? In front of other people? Never mind the time commitment. By late 2016, I'd gotten remarried, had a full-time job, and was busy co-parenting my twelve-year-old daughter and ten-year-old son with my ex. Then a local community theater announced their spring show. *Wizard of Oz*. Yes, that's correct. *Wizard. Of. Oz.* My brain rewound thirty years. I trembled every time the Wicked Witch appeared on screen. I cried every time Dorothy said goodbye to her friends. I knew all the songs backward and forward. I had to audition.

I prepared by listening to "Thank You for The Music" on repeat for weeks. Who am I kidding? I already knew it by heart. I'd only seen *Mamma Mia!* four times already. On a cold night at the end of February, I drove to the barn. Yes, I said barn. This theater company rehearsed in a gutted barn. Luckily, it didn't smell like one. The big open room was more like an elementary school gym. I sat on a folding chair and waited my turn to sing.

"Jaimie," I heard my name called.

"Yes." I confidently walked over to the director's table where he sat with his team.

"Ready?" the director asked.

"As I'll ever be." I laughed. But I wasn't.

Composing myself, I belted out the song as best I could, while my legs quivered underneath me. Afterward, I smiled, thanked them, and returned to my freezing metal seat. By the time my resting heart rate settled, it was time to learn some choreography. I joined the other folks who were also auditioning and waited for instructions. No nerves there. That was the fun part. I was ready for that. My drum corps color guard instructors had taught me well.

On the drive home, my mind raced like a hamster wheel. Had I sounded good enough in the vocal audition? Had they noticed my toes weren't pointed in that last split leap? As soon as I got home, the mental and physical exhaustion took over. I was asleep in minutes.

The next morning, before I cleared the cobwebs out of my eyes, I clicked on the theater's web page to check for updates.

Nothing.

Ugh. What was taking them so long? No. I don't do patient. Thanks for asking. By the afternoon, I told myself I wasn't getting a part. But when I looked again, I saw my name on the screen underneath "Callback."

They wanted to see me again to read for the part of the Wicked Witch.

My jaw almost hit the keyboard. I pumped both fists in the air and shouted "Yes" to no one in particular. Working alone at home did have its drawbacks.

The following night, I sneered at the entire creative team and gave them my best cackle. I strutted out of the barn feeling good about it—only to hear nothing back. The full cast list didn't include my name.

Now wait one damn minute.

I had potential to be the Wicked Witch. That's what a callback meant, right? I understood others were better the night before. But wasn't I even good enough to be in the chorus? My face felt hot. Then the sad truth settled in my gut. No, I wasn't good enough. My eyes burned and I willed myself to not cry. I tried to tell myself it wasn't meant to be.

And that life goes on.

A few days later, the phone rang as I set the table for dinner. I didn't know the number but decided to live dangerously and answer it.

"Hi, Jaimie! Could you come to the first rehearsal?"

I recognized the voice of the *Wizard of Oz*'s director. Confused, the gears turned in my brain. What rehearsal? I couldn't form words.

"Someone forgot to call you. I'm so sorry. We'd like to offer you a spot in the ensemble. Can you join us at the barn tonight?"

"As in now?" I asked.

"Umm, yeah."

The first rehearsal was in progress as we spoke. My heart pounded. Could I drop everything and go? That wasn't me. Not being the planner that I was. I muted the phone, still not really believing I'd gotten a part, and quickly recapped the call to my husband.

"Yes! Go!" he blurted out.

"I'll be there soon. Thank you so much," I said and hung up.

I ran to my room, changed into comfy clothes, and raced back into the dining room to tell the kids. "I'm in the show! I need to go to rehearsal right now."

The kids cheered.

Bopping from one to the other, I gave them each a quick kiss on their heads, then hopped into the car.

From that moment on, there was no looking back. Two or three nights a week, the barn was my second home. My eyes sparkled as I watched the leads run their scenes. Sometimes, I leaned against the wall and chitchatted with other cast members, but not loud enough to get yelled at by the director. That was the teens. I gravitated toward one special woman, Joann, the only other female in my age group.

Somehow, at the end of rehearsal one night, we got onto the topic of mammograms. After hitting the big 4-0 earlier that year, I thought it was something I should do. I didn't need to be talked into it, but I also didn't have a sense of urgency about it. She *strongly* encouraged me to go. I trusted her and knew she was looking out for me. Plus, when the last "Go!" had treated me so well, who was I to argue with this one?

JUST MARK IT

Calm and empowered, I drove to the clinic for my first mammogram. I was being proactive. That had to count for something. I didn't love feeling my boob squished and pinched to the size of a silver-dollar pancake. But then I wasn't expecting it to be comfortable. It was part of the dues women paid to stay healthy.

The next day, I got the call. "We found something abnormal," the nurse told me.

My mouth went dry. My brain felt like a scrambled egg. My own body had betrayed me.

"The next step is a needle biopsy," she explained. "We need to figure out what we're dealing with."

"Okay." Stunned, I scheduled the procedure for two days later.

Could I seriously have breast cancer? No. Not fair. I hadn't seen or felt any lumps. I was barely forty. I wasn't okay with this at all. Over the next forty-eight hours, I became my best friend and worst enemy.

Angel on my shoulder: You're fine, it's not cancer.

Devil on my other shoulder: That's it, you have cancer, and it's spread throughout your body. You might as well start planning the funeral while you can.

The morning of the biopsy, I tried to calm my nerves. "It's just another doctor appointment," I told myself. But I knew deep down it wasn't. First of all, I'd driven to the hospital rather than to the clinic. From there, I was directed to the cancer center, where I was given a pink gown and a key to a locker for my clothes. I sat in the waiting room, eyeing the women around me with a mixture of fear and pity.

Unlike the mammogram, this procedure hurt like a *bitch*. "This is going to feel like a bee sting" my ass. I mean, she stabbed my breast with a gigantic needle. Good thing the nurses didn't mind my colorful language. I bit my lip as tears slid down my face.

When it was over, I sat up and pulled the paper-thin gown tighter around me, trying to focus on the important details about taking care of myself post-procedure.

"Here are two gel ice packs. These and pain relievers will be your best friends." The nurse handed me two bright pink ice packs.

Was I sensing a theme here? "Thank you. Is there anything else to watch?"

"If you have a fever, call this number immediately," she added.

"Got it," I assured her.

"Also, no lifting anything over five pounds."

Cheers once again for being done with my newborn-parenting phase.

"And no strenuous activity, like running or jogging," she finished.

Wait. What about *Oz* rehearsal? I couldn't jazz run, but I could mark through the steps, right? I answered that question myself, went home, and changed for rehearsal.

Off to the barn I went—with ice packs stuffed into my sports bra.

Throughout the night, I took multiple trips to the freezer to rotate those ice packs so they stayed cold. I hadn't said anything to the director. Why would I? But my multiple "exit stage rights" definitely piqued the curiosity of a couple women in the kitchen. I lowered my voice to barely louder than a whisper. "I had a needle biopsy today, and I'm supposed to keep the area cold."

The head costumer's eyes welled up. "Breast cancer?"

"Maybe. Hopefully, I'll know for sure soon."

She gave me a hug, careful not to squeeze too hard. "Would you share news when you have it?"

"Of course." Back to rehearsal I went.

I kept busy after that. I needed to do my job. I drove my kids to and from school. Busy-mom life came in handy while I waited.

The nurse called a few days later. "The results are benign!" She got right to the point. "You don't have cancer."

My heart exploded with gratitude, my brain and mouth stopped working together, and I loudly let all the air out of my lungs.

"The abnormalities were simply calcifications," she explained further. "But to be safe, come back in a year."

"Of course," I promised. I could do that. No problem. "Thank you for calling," I said through my biggest smile.

The rest of the day, my fingers tapped away at my work emails. I was healthy, and they weren't going to write themselves.

FIVE, 6, 7, 8!

After several weeks of barn rehearsals, the cast and crew moved to the performing arts center at the local high school. I stepped inside, and the theme song from *The Jefferson's* played in my head. The facility was gorgeous. I wouldn't need to squeeze around Auntie Em's house anymore. I'd be able to do the choreography full-out and not worry about kicking another cast member. I sat in a cushy seat watching the leads run their scenes as we all buckled up for hell week . . . I mean tech week.

Thursday's "invited dress rehearsal" kicked off four shows in four days. I knew someone in the audience during every performance and soaked up every exhilarating and exhausting moment. The following day, I felt like I'd been run over by a truck. And it was absolutely worth it.

Bitten by the theater bug, I dreamed about being in another show. I wanted to do it all over again. When the theater announced *Joseph and the Amazing Technicolor Dreamcoat*, I shrugged. I'd heard of the musical but didn't know any of the songs. I'd have to learn them. Why would I want to do that? Because I'd get to sing and dance again. I wrote the audition dates on the family whiteboard.

On audition day, I walked back into the barn with a little bit of swagger. I had a theater résumé now. I smiled at the creative team, introduced myself, and pressed play to sing along on my phone.

And a commercial started.

Beads of sweat formed on my forehead, but I tried not to let them show. Quick on my feet, I made a joke. "Today, I'll be singing about car insurance."

That garnered a collective chuckle from the table.

I sang a bunch of bars from a Billy Joel song and returned to my folding chair to impatiently wait for the group choreography.

Josh introduced himself as our choreographer.

I already knew him by name. We had friends in common, and he'd directed several shows for our community theater. "Okay, line up here." Wasting no time, he taught sixteen counts of choreography for "Go, Go, Go Joseph."

Smiling from ear to ear, I couldn't wait to work with him. Luckily, cast as one of the wives, I didn't have to wait long.

I looked forward to every rehearsal with Josh. His choreography pushed the limits of my talent, but I was proud to achieve his vision. He did the steps along with us. We all sweated in that barn together. And he was funny as hell. At some point during every rehearsal, I laughed. I really liked him. As far as I could tell, he liked me too. Or at the very least, he respected my dance skills.

One blistering hot afternoon, he called me out in the middle of the rehearsal. "Jaimie, I need to run this part with the guys. Will you run it outside with the ladies?"

"Of course. I'm on it." I jumped up and ran out the door, thrilled to have that extra responsibility. I was also grateful to have a break from the stuffy barn. I didn't have a thermometer, but I was sure it was a solid ten degrees cooler outside. Even with box fans on full blast, we were all melting in there.

A few rehearsals later, Josh named me as one of the dance captains for the show. I knew he was still the choreographer and in an authority position, but I felt like we were becoming friends. We spent some time together outside of rehearsal. We had our own private jokes. After the last performance, I cried nonstop. I was going to miss this group of people so much. And I wasn't sure when I would see Josh next.

A couple weeks later, my phone buzzed with a text.

Josh: Do you want to be a backup dancer in a drag show pageant?

I didn't even know drag show pageants existed. In fact, I'd never seen a drag show in my life. Not even one episode of *RuPaul's Drag Race.* But my friend was asking for my help on stage. How could I say no?

Me: OMG, yes!

On a beautiful sunny Saturday afternoon in October, my husband and I made our way over to FIVE Nightclub for the first rehearsal. Josh had asked him to be a backup dancer too. FIVE was minutes from our house, and I'd never even heard of it.

As I walked in, a sense of deep comfort washed over me, and I thought of my brother Cory. Six years earlier, blood cancer had taken him from the world and from me. He'd owned a cleaning company with a few bars as clients. I'd helped him more than once. Now I was at this club to help Josh with his work.

Michael, Jacob, and Dan—the other backup dancers—introduced themselves politely and professionally. We got right to work. The Katy Perry/Lady Gaga megamix blasted through the club's speakers, and Josh walked through the choreography. The first rehearsal had the perfect mix of focus and fun. In a couple hours, I felt connected to Michael, Jacob, and Dan. They were hilarious, dramatic, and hell-bent on seeing our queen, Beverly Bee, take the crown.

We spent weeks learning and rehearsing the choreography. One day, FIVE wasn't available for rehearsal, and I offered up our house. We had plenty of room in the basement. We knew the steps. Now we needed to sell the number. I lost count of how many times we ran it that afternoon. We didn't want any surprises during the pageant, so we wore part of our costumes. The swatch of fabric was the size of a bandana. I found sequins in the tub drain for months after and smiled every time.

A week later, I attended my first drag show. At FIVE, naturally. Haley, another backup dancer for Beverly and a *Joseph* cast member, invited me. She worked for a local nonprofit that hosted an annual drag show benefit. The theme was Superheroes vs. Villains. Costumes were strongly encouraged. I had to play along, right? So, I squeezed into a full body purple unitard. Obviously, I owned a purple unitard. I grew up in the 80s after all and knew it would come in handy someday. Thanks again, Goodwill. I pulled on a pair of black bikini bottoms, painted a mask with black eye shadow, and pretended I was a superhero.

I will be forever grateful for that invite. I walked into the bar, equal parts unsure of what to expect and so excited I almost peed my pants. The smell of popcorn almost knocked me over. In the very best way. I felt joy radiating from the crowd. The place was packed.

Seconds into the first song, I stood on my tiptoes to see the first performer. *Where had this been my entire life?*

A male entertainer kicked off the show. The screams from the audience were deafening as he gyrated on stage in a skin-tight unitard. His strategically placed mesh cutouts left little to the imagination.

The first queen danced onto the stage. Balanced on four-inch heels, her wig brushed up against the ceiling. Her thick, luscious eyelashes batted at me from across the room. The gown belonged at a Vanity Fair Oscar party.

Every queen who performed exuded confidence and fun in her own way. A tight horseshoe of fans surrounded the stage, arms outstretched with dollar bills. I didn't want the night to end.

Pageant night felt different. I was excited, but also nervous. I had a job to do—help Beverly bring home the crown of Wisconsin Entertainer of the Year. Her individual talent number was from *Into the Woods*. The crowd went wild as she channeled Meryl Streep's Witch.

The competing queens also brought their A games. I really didn't know how the night would end. As the pageant performers dwindled before Beverly's main number, the other backup dancers and I casually left the table one at a time. We met backstage and squeezed each other's hands. We knew what to do. We were ready.

The audience didn't know what hit them. No one expected six backup dancers. The audience screamed throughout our entire performance. We all stayed and watched the other queens perform, waiting until the wee hours to find out who would be crowned.

The announcer took the stage, flashed a dazzling smile, and winked at the audience.

In anticipation, we all perched on the edge of our seats, collectively holding our breath.

"The 2017 Entertainer of the Year is . . ." Drum roll, please. "BEVERLY BEE!"

I needed this energy to be a regular part of my life. I considered Michael, Dan, and Jacob to be new friends. We forged a bond through sweat, sequins, and heavy eye makeup. Somewhere along the way, I learned that they performed in drag as Emilay, Lucy, and Kayos. I followed them all on social media. Basically, I became a groupie. If one of them was hosting or performing in a show, my butt was in the audience.

While I was having a blast with my new friends that fall, my friend Sarah found out she had Acute Myeloid Leukemia (AML). Her diagnosis punched me in the gut. Our kids went to grade school together, and she was one of the kindest human beings I'd ever met. I knew all too well that I couldn't cure her. But I needed to do something. It had been years since I'd personally fundraised for cancer research. Sarah changed that. Since my very first drag show had been a fundraising benefit, why not host one? A couple months after the pageant, I asked Josh if Beverly Bee would be my host. And, without a second of hesitation, she was in.

Between going to drag shows regularly and having my own drag show benefit in the works for a cause I cared deeply about, I was living my best life—until Josh got offered a job across the country. I had a series of reactions. *Noooooo, you can't move! I'm going to miss you too much* which turned into *I'm so happy for you* and ended with *Ummm, who's going to choreograph for the next youth musical*, another cause I felt strongly about.

A year earlier, my daughter had joined this amazing theater program that empowered kids with different abilities to star in modified Broadway musicals. It warmed my heart to see the way they worked together. I clapped and cheered from the audience. When the entire cast performed a final song together, I blubbered well past the final note. I'd been so excited for her second season to see how Josh would choreograph the show. But now he was leaving.

Feeling bold after I finished up my pity party, I sent an email to the creative team offering to help with choreography. By that point, I'd been in a couple musicals and had years of informal dance training behind me. Surely, I could pitch in. And before you could say five-six-seven-eight, I was a co-choreographer.

As I prepared to say goodbye to Josh, it hit me like a ton of bricks. I didn't have a drag show benefit host anymore. I sure as hell couldn't host it myself. Out at FIVE one night, I brought this up to him.

With zero hesitation, he replied, "Ask Lucy to host." He walked over to her and put her on the spot.

Incredible human that she was, her answer was, "Yes!"

Josh moved away. And life moved on. I folded in choreographer rehearsals two or three days a week along with fabulous drag shows, and now I really was living the dream.

BACK IN A YEAR

Every winter I spent in Madison, I questioned why I lived in the Midwest. My back ached from shoveling snow. I couldn't feel my fingers when it dropped below fifty degrees. And then my sinuses double-crossed me. My head felt like a balloon. I wanted to bash my cheekbones with a hammer. Late in the winter of 2017, I finally went to see the doctor.

After examining me for three minutes, he said, "Hmmm, it looks like you have a sinus infection."

"I know. I've struggled with them since high school," I replied.

"You know the drill. Antibiotics, water, and rest."

As I checked out of the clinic and discussed follow-up appointments, a light bulb went off in my head. I was supposed to have another mammogram. I scheduled it for the beginning of April.

My husband and I drove to New York City with the kids for spring break. It was my daughter's second time there and my son's first. We took too many pictures in a wax museum in Times Square. And naturally stopped at Levain Bakery. It was physically impossible for me to be in New York and not go. We sat on the floor of Grand Central Station with Jen, her partner Kobi, and so many baked goods from Magnolia Bakery that my stomach hurt looking at them. We had such a blast, I almost forgot my appointment when we got back home. As terrified as I'd been the year prior, I wasn't worried at all this time around. It was nothing the last time. It would be fine.

I had the mammogram in the middle of the day and went right back to work. End of story. Or so I thought.

The next day a nurse called. "Unfortunately, the results of your mammogram weren't clear."

"Oh. Okay," I murmured. What did that mean exactly?

"I'm so sorry, but we're going to need to do another one," she informed me.

Okayyyy, fine.

After the second mammogram, I got another phone call from the nurse. "We found something. The doctor would like to do a biopsy."

Well shit. Another "bee sting" to my breast. That's when I started to get a little nervous. My heart beat a little faster as I not only anticipated the pain but also a potential diagnosis. Okay. I took a deep breath. I'd had a biopsy before. It could still be nothing. I could do this.

I was less traumatized by my second biopsy. Don't get me wrong—it still hurt. But I expected the pain. I knew how to take care of myself afterward. I found security in past experience and knowledge.

A few days later, I sat at my desk responding to work emails when a number I recognized popped up on my phone. My throat tightened.

"We have the results from your biopsy," the nurse said.

After what felt like the longest pause of my life—which probably lasted a total of one second—she said, "There's cancer."

My heart took off like an Olympian sprinter, my head went fuzzy, and my heart sank all the way to my stomach. I tried so hard to take in everything she was saying, but all I could say was "okay" over and over again. The part I did get was that the surgeon had an opening and could see me the next day. Lucky, right?

The one thing I remember from that appointment was Dr. Dulick's kindness. No, not doctor. Nathan. Okay, make that two things. He didn't want to be called Dr. Dulick. Growing up, every adult had either Mr./Mrs./Dr. or aunt/uncle before their name. My mom had one sister, yet I can think of ten "aunts" off the top of my head. How could I possibly call my surgeon by his first name? But my mom also taught me respect, and he wanted me to call him Nathan, so I did.

His extreme kindness soothed my heart. He took his time explaining my diagnosis. "One year ago, there were three calcifications." He pointed to his computer monitor. "These two together, and this separate one. That's the one we biopsied." He double clicked the mouse. "This is your most recent scan."

The three small dots transformed into a giant constellation.

"From one year to the next, this is not a subtle change," he continued.

I didn't like the sound of that.

"This is one of the larger changes I've seen in my sixteen years practicing medicine."

Now was when I had to be an overachiever? Screw that.

"You can take a picture with your phone if you like," he offered.

Those pictures later helped me explain my diagnosis to my entire family, who lived across the country. But for the time being, I kept the news to myself.

After that appointment, my head felt clearer than it had in days. I had answers. I was done white knuckling test taking and waiting for results. Oh, wait, no I wasn't. While we knew there was cancer in my breast, Nathan wanted to see if it had spread to my lymph nodes.

Spoiler alert—it had.

At least I enjoyed a distraction as I waited for those test results. Four days after the first time I met with Nathan, I sat down with Lucy at FIVE to discuss plans for our benefit. She told me about the upcoming fundraiser show she'd be hosting. They had a family-friendly show earlier in the evening and a main show later. Ours would be the same format. If my teenager couldn't come and bring her friends, why even host? Since neither my parents nor my children knew about my diagnosis, I definitely wasn't sharing that information with Lucy. And if I had anything to say about it, the benefit would happen no matter what.

Luckily for me, Lucy knew how to plan a benefit. I asked Emilay, Kayos, and Haley to perform in the show, and they graciously accepted. Lucy booked the rest of the cast and took care of the details. Which was great, because I had a few other things on my mind.

Given the overachiever I was when it came to the rate of my cancer's growth, Nathan encouraged genetic testing. The blood draw barely took any time at all. Waiting for the results, though? Felt like an eternity.

Weeks later, I got my answer. I tested positive for the CHEK2 genetic mutation. BRCA I'd heard of. Hadn't most of the world, thanks to Angelina Jolie? But I had no idea what the hell CHEK2 was about. I sat down with a kind, professional genetic testing expert who showed me page after page of numbers. The only number I needed to know? Thirty.

There was a thirty percent chance I would at some point be diagnosed with cancer in my other breast. THIRTY PERCENT? Nope. No way. Not taking that chance. Not willing to wait year after year for another diagnosis, I decided to say goodbye to both my breasts.

Days later, I met with a plastic surgeon. I waited for Dr. Lake in a gown and pair of leggings. Having read up on plastic surgery beforehand, I understood my two choices on the most basic level.

CHOICE A: Breast implants

CHOICE B: Take some fat from another part of my body to help give me breasts again.

For most people, it might not even be a choice. Take some of my fat? Sign me up. Only, in the irony of it all, I didn't have the extra fat. Slender my whole life, my high school friends had teased me for being too skinny. I opened the robe for the doctor, and she shook her head. I weighed more than I ever had but apparently not enough for the procedure. Could I at least have a margarita to go along with the salt in that wound?

I had a decision to make. Did I want implants or not? I made two lists.

IMPLANTS:
- I don't want to be flat.
- Will I "need" to get all new clothes?
- Will I feel deformed if I don't have reconstruction?
- I'm already self-conscious having a small chest.

- With reconstruction, I will feel more like myself.
- What if I wear prosthetics and they ride up all the time? Or look weird?

FLAT & FABULOUS:

- Maybe I won't mind being flat?
- Will I have back pain with the implants?
- Do I really want more surgeries and recovery time?
- Who cares if you're flat?
- If it seems too good to be true, maybe it is.
- I've said for so long, "I'm not getting implants."
- If my expectation is looking "perfect," will I be disappointed if I don't?
- What if I go bigger and don't like looking bigger?
- I won't feel any sensation with implants. You've got to be kidding me.

My brain flip-flopped with each competing thought. I tortured my best friends, arguing through my options in their chat boxes. My treatment plan after surgery included chemotherapy and radiation. The plastic surgeon flat-out refused immediate reconstruction. If I wanted to go that route, I had to wait a year.

I kept thinking about the summer—my favorite time of year in Madison. After twenty weeks of chemotherapy, six weeks of radiation, and healing time, would I really want to spend my summer in surgery so I could have "breasts"?

Another spoiler alert—I did not.

And I very much enjoyed that summer completely free of surgeries, thank you very much.

PROUD LESBIAN CHICK

An ally of the LGBTQIA+ community for as long as I can remember, I'd never attended Pride festivities. As a straight, cisgender woman, I didn't think I had a right to be there. But in June 2018, my daughter and I hit Milwaukee's PrideFest with a couple queer friends. Imagine an outdoor job fair . . . then cover it in rainbows and glitter.

I visited so many tables that day, but a charity walk I'd done fifteen years earlier in memory of my Uncle Chuck jumped out at me. As I visited with the staff about the previous spokespeople, a pair of clear blue eyes from the promo poster propped on the table pierced my soul. Matt Bomer. My #1 guy crush. And the spokesperson for the upcoming walk.

Before I knew it, I scribbled my name on a sheet requesting more information. Maybe my daughter and I could fundraise and walk together. Not long after, I got a couple postcards with Mr. Bomer's chiseled jawline and something along the lines of *Are you sure you don't want to register?* Okay, stop badgering me already. Done. Registered.

I didn't plan on raising much money. I mean, there was this pesky cancer to deal with. But if I raised even one dollar, that would help. At the very least, I'd generate awareness for the charity.

A few weeks later, I received a letter in the mail. It promised that every person who raised $1,000 would be able to take a picture with Matt at the walk. Wait, what? A picture of us? Standing next to each other? In real life? That did it. Get ready for a grand coming your way, charity walk. But please stand by while I recover from minor surgery first.

Four days after my double mastectomy, I told my husband I wanted to go to the MadCity Drag Revue. I mean, I could continue to sit in my house, or I could get in the car and sit at a table at FIVE. Sitting was sitting. Never one to turn down a night out, he agreed.

I didn't even bother to change. I wasn't going to walk the runway at a fashion show. I'd been wearing my teenager's plaid button-down shirt since I'd left the hospital. It hurt to even think about pulling a shirt over my head. Feeling as crusty as the shirt, I walked carefully into FIVE. I didn't want to bust any stitches. I eyed two seats and sat down without making a sound. I felt out of place.

Bryanna sashayed onto the stage and introduced herself as the host. I'd been to enough drag shows that I knew her name, but we hadn't officially met. That night, I was starstruck by her. Her make-up was on point and her wig perfectly styled. Her dress hugged her curves flawlessly. I felt a pang of jealousy as I thought about the bandages covering the scars across my chest wall. Then the music pulsed through the speakers, and I only felt joy.

At the halfway point of the show, she picked on various audience members. Before long, her gaze landed on my husband. No surprise there. Over the course of our relationship, I lost count how many times someone asked me if he was gay. There was a reason I called him my "gay straight boyfriend" before we were married. "And who are you here with?" she asked him.

"My wife," he replied.

Bryanna's gaze moved to me. "You're pretty! Like, really pretty."

And . . . start the ugly crying. Well, only in my imagination. But after Bryanna professed my beauty in front of everyone, I added her show to my calendar.

After a few weeks of recovery, I prepared for chemotherapy. Every other Friday for eight weeks, Adriamycin and Cytoxan coursed throughout my body. Taxol followed every week for twelve weeks. My oncologist informed me my hair would fall out ten days or so into treatment. I decided to be proactive. One super short haircut coming up.

My daughter's reaction to the cut? "You look like a lesbian."

I had no words but almost fell down laughing.

Sure enough, my oncologist knew what he was talking about. Ten days after my first treatment, clumps of my hair littered the shower. I was disgusted. No, thank you. Pass. I asked my daughter if she wanted to buzz my hair. She was thrilled. While I leaned over the edge of the tub, she worked her magic. The last time I had hair that short, I was a baby. After that, she and her brother called me their baby chick for months.

WIGS

Six weeks after my surgery and three weeks after starting chemotherapy, I co-hosted my first drag show benefit. No need for the baby chick to make an appearance that night. I already had a wig in mind. The same purple wig I'd worn when I'd cheered on other fundraisers. Purple equaled powerful.

To keep the color theme going, I paired it with a purple sequined dress. Doesn't every woman wear sequins when in a gay bar? The last time I'd worn that dress was with Jen in New York City the night she introduced me to *Flaming Saddles*. We were the only two women in a bar full of hot men, tight chaps, and cowboy boots. How it took so long for gay bars to become a standard part of my life was beyond me.

The scoop of my neckline wasn't too low, so I wore my bra and prosthetics. Since my diagnosis, I'd followed my doctor's suggestions, and that seemed to be working well for me. Wearing prosthetics was part of the deal now. I will give credit for the convincing appearance. Just pop two cutlets into the bra and you're back to your old self. If only it been that easy in middle school.

One of my friends came up to me between the early and late shows. After catching up for a few minutes, she asked if I'd had my surgery yet.

Pointing to my chest, I said, "Yes, girl! The display case is empty."

I floated back to my table for the second half of the benefit. I screamed and clapped during every performance. At the end of the show, Lucy called me up to the stage. When we planned the show, we agreed the door charge was for the charity. The performers could keep their tips. Lucy thanked everyone for coming, and me for putting the show together. Before I knew what was happening, the performers all threw handfuls of cash toward me. My face lit up as I felt the money shower over me. They decided to give their tips to the charity too. In total, the benefit raised over $1,000 for cancer research. Not too shabby for a first-timer three weeks into cancer treatment.

A week later, my medical team suggested I visit the wig salon at the hospital. For most of my life, I'd rocked long hair. Minus that bowl cut when I was seven. Thanks, Mom. And one sassy short cut after college. Thanks, *The Limited* model. While I lived my best baby chick life, I embraced head scarves. I wore hats inside if the air conditioning was on. But at the end of the day, I missed my hair. Honestly, many days I missed my hair more than I missed my breasts.

My health insurance covered one wig. At the salon, I met with an incredibly kind human who let me try on wig after wig. She took pictures and waited while I texted them to my sister and my best friend. Knowing that I was going to be sporting one look for a good stretch of time, I felt like I had to choose very carefully. I ended up picking long brown, wavy hair. Very Carrie Bradshaw in the first *Sex and the City* movie. It was gorgeous—luscious, really—and deserved its own special debut.

My husband and I had bought *Waitress* tickets months before. My friend Joann and her husband made it a double date.

We met at a local hole-in-the wall Mexican restaurant before the show. With pitchers of margaritas, we celebrated life and friendship. The perfect night for a wig debut. Grateful to look somewhat like my pre-cancer self, that wig was everything I wanted it to be.

It was also a couple things I didn't want it to be. Insanely hot and itchy for starters. I felt like I was bursting into flames. How did the queens wear them? And for hours on end? I decided to wear it on special occasions only, which turned out to be two weddings and my teenager's musical. I left it off at home, which doubled as my workplace. After a while, I stopped wearing it at FIVE too. Underneath their fabulous wigs, those queens didn't have much more hair than I did. And none of them seemed to care. When I was there, I might as well have been at home anyway.

A WINNER, BABY!

Overall, my cancer journey progressed smoothly. I tolerated chemotherapy every Friday. By Friday night, I felt waves of nausea. But I didn't throw up. I counted that as a huge win. I listened to my body. I rested when I got tired. My bosses at the nonprofit where I worked were great about that, trusting me to do my job.

One summer afternoon, I felt like total garbage and laid down. But simply going horizontal didn't cut it. Around three o'clock, I finally broke down and called the nurse. "I don't know what's wrong, but I don't feel well," I whimpered.

"Have you vomited?" the nurse asked.

"No, I haven't thrown up in a long time." I was happy to report that at least.

"Do you have a fever?" she asked.

"Umm, I don't know. I didn't check. I never get fevers, even when I'm really sick," I explained.

"If you've felt this bad for hours, I suggest you go to the ER to get checked out. The clinic will be closing soon," she informed me.

"Do I haaaaave to?" I whined.

"It's your choice what you do next, but I really think you should go to the emergency room," she said more sternly.

I hung up the phone, cried for a bit, then drove myself to the ER. Yes, I can be stubborn about being strong and taking care of myself.

When I got there, the nurse drew blood to see if I was neutropenic. Quick definition to save you an online search. Neutrophils are a type of white blood cell that help heal damaged tissues and fight infections. Yeahhhhh, chemo also kills them along with the good cells you'd rather keep. If I was low on neutrophils, that meant my immune system sucked. And that wasn't good. Cancer patients don't just get sick. They get dangerously sick.

But . . . yay . . . not neutropenic. Still, my blood needed refreshing. I mentally prepared for my first blood transfusion. Fresh blood pumped through me overnight, and I left by noon the next day. Blood transfusions were no big deal.

Until they were.

Weeks later, my oncologist prescribed iron pills. I wasn't surprised, I'd struggled with anemia since college. The pills were no joke. In a matter of days, I became really constipated. Then the pain took over. Desperate, I tried all the suggested remedies. I drank more water. I choked down prune juice. I ate more fiber. I took over-the-counter meds. Nothing. Frustrated and defeated, I called the cancer center after-hours care line.

"You're doing all the right things," the nurse said. "Your next step is magnesium citrate. You can buy it over the counter. I'm going to warn you. It can really clean you out."

I gulped. I was simultaneously scared and repulsed.

"If the magnesium citrate doesn't help, go to the hospital."

I drove to a local pharmacy and couldn't find the magnesium citrate. I took a deep breath and headed for the consultation window. "Hi, I can't seem to find magnesium citrate."

"I'm sorry, we're out of stock," the pharmacist explained.

I felt like screaming. How could they be out of stock? Did they know how much pain I was in? Before I could formulate a response, I broke down crying.

"Let me call another pharmacy for you. I'll ask them to hold a bottle."

"Thank you so much. I usually don't cry in public like this." I wiped my eye, walked back to my car, and drove straight to the other pharmacy. Sure enough, the solution was waiting for me behind the counter. I thanked the pharmacist profusely and power-walked back to my car.

I followed the directions on the bottle to the letter. My pain only increased. I sat in a few inches of warm water in the tub crying, willing my body to cooperate. I felt like I was in labor.

"Can I do anything?" my husband yelled from the other room.

I didn't answer. If I knew, wouldn't I have asked already? Maybe you could get your ass off the couch, set down your phone for a bit, and check on me from the same room. Simple suggestion.

I barely slept that night. Early the next morning, I grimaced as I got dressed. ER, here I come. Probably for another blood transfusion. I informed my husband of my plans.

"Do you want me to take you?" he asked.

"No, I can drive." Sure, I was in pain, but we lived ten minutes from the hospital. I was admitted and grit my teeth through yet another blood draw. My labs showed neutropenia. Dammit. That changed things. I called my husband to let him know.

"Do you want me to come?" he asked.

"No, that's okay. Go ahead with your day." An all-day ER visit didn't exactly mesh with his plans for a 10th anniversary yard-game tournament with a large group of close friends. He'd never missed one.

While he played bocce ball and ladder toss, I sobbed in pain. The terrible constipation caused hemorrhoids. Yet another new experience for me. The ER doctor prescribed meds to clean out my system as well as antibiotics to fight the infection. *Rough* combination. I bawled every time I went to the bathroom that day. Relief between crying fits came in the form of a tablet. My best friend KG and her family gifted me one for treatment. That day I turned it on for comfort and binged the entire first season of *Insatiable*.

I also leaned on my nurse. Hard. He checked on me often. He held my arm to walk me to the bathroom and even applied ointment afterward. Normally, I'd be too proud or embarrassed to accept that kind of help. Nope, not that day.

Around dinnertime, my husband came to visit. "Everyone was asking about you."

DUH. Maybe because your friends were wondering why you weren't here with me.

"But here's the best part," he said. "Scott and I won the whole tournament and the cash prize. We won it for you."

Were you freaking kidding me? I wanted to punch him in the face. He quite literally won his day, and I'd lost mine. Yes, he'd asked me if I wanted him there. But really? Why was it ever a question?

MY DAY

Call me Miss Planner. Please. I've managed the calendar for my entire family for years. I was also a big believer in birthdays. I drew hearts and confetti on the huge white board in our kitchen. Every birthday deserved to be celebrated. Maybe not with a petting zoo. I wasn't that extra. But I did think that for one day the birthday person should be made to feel special. The kids always chose the family dinner and dessert. My husband got more. I took time off from work to spend the day with him. Two different years, I planned a party for him—one a surprise, the other a joint effort.

My birthdays arrived with less fanfare. Who wanted to plan their own party, right? My last pre-cancer birthday came and went with zero celebration. I was beyond frustrated. Days after, my husband and I walked around the neighborhood for hours. I explained how I felt about birthdays. I really wanted him to take the lead with mine. Not plan a bash with hundreds of my closest friends, necessarily, but at least start the conversation. At the very least, ask me how I wanted to spend my special day.

But in the month leading up to my birthday, I got nothing. My birthday was blank on the calendar. There wasn't even something that could serve as a surprise party placeholder. I refused to ask him any questions about my special day. Him taking initiative was the whole point of the conversation we'd had. And if he had been planning something, I didn't want to ask and spoil my own surprise party. I held out hope. But deep down, I was nauseated every time I thought about it.

Leaving the weekend before my birthday open, I made zero plans. An entire empty weekend? Unheard of for me. As each day crept closer, my anxiety spiked. Finally over it, I put my poor best friend on the spot. "I know I might be spoiling something, but I'm losing my mind. Do you know if he's planning something?"

"I don't know of anything," KG answered.

My heart jumped to my throat. I wanted so much to be wrong about him. I was ready and willing to eat humble pie.

That Thursday, my friend Trisha posted on social media complaining that no one wanted to go to the Indigo Girls concert with her. First of all, what? Second, she needed to find new friends. Stat. I commented on this travesty, and she invited me to join her. Should I say yes? What if that was the night of my big surprise party?

I messaged my husband, and he immediately replied with, "Go! What a fun early treat for your birthday."

Wait, wait, wait. True, it would be a fun treat. But did he think he was off the hook? Because that was not what I meant. That was him 100% not taking the lead.

That Saturday night, Trisha and I enjoyed a fantastic concert. Icons, those Indigo Girls. They sang "Closer to Fine" near the end of the show. I sang along until my voice broke. Nowhere near fine, tears streamed down my cheeks.

At the end of the weekend, the husband mentioned my birthday for the second time. "I have a day off this week. I was thinking I could come with you to chemo and take you to lunch."

My heart sank. Ten months into the worst year of my life and now he offered to go with me? I'd never asked for his company for a reason. I didn't love losing my hair or the waves of nausea. But I actually enjoyed my time in the treatment room. An extrovert who worked from home, I craved time with other people. I loved my nurses who'd become my friends. As for his suggestion of lunch afterward, talk about extra effort. Whoa there. Don't go all out or anything.

That Friday, I walked into the private treatment room ahead of him. I couldn't believe it. My favorite nurse had decorated the window area. Shimmery banner letters spelled "Happy Birthday" next to crepe paper streamers. She'd taped a picture of Matt Bomer to the glass and written the words, *Hey girl . . . I hear it's your birthday. I hope it is amazing just like you.* She'd remembered my favorite star, for crying out loud.

This woman, who I'd known only a few months, did more for me that day than my husband. You could've heard a pin drop in the room. We sat in opposite corners, both occupied by our phones the entire time. Only the beeps from the IV machines pierced the silence. It didn't make sense. I hadn't asked him to read my mind. I'd told him flat out *my birthday is important to me.*

We went to lunch afterward at one of my favorite places in town. Hurt and confused, I ordered a boozy shake and finally broke the silence. "This is all we're doing for my birthday then?"

He exploded and threw his hands in the air. "Your standards are so high, they're presidential. I feel like I can never do anything good enough for you, so why even try?"

Like a backhand across my face, his words knocked the wind out of me. Unable to speak, I sat there crying into my drink while he ate his lunch, my brain filling with judgments. About me, not him. Stupid, right? But not at the time. Not where I was at emotionally. Not where we were at in our marriage. All I could think was that maybe my standards were too high. That I did ask too much of him. That I was a terrible, unreasonable person.

Not exactly the special day I'd hoped for. Maybe next year would be better.

ELEVEN

Finally, it was almost time for the charity walk, and I hustled to raise that thousand dollars. *I'm so ready for that picture, Matt!* I'd needed something to look forward to during treatment.

A few days before the event, the phone rang, and I gave the 262 area code a chance.

"I'm calling to inform you that Mr. Bomer will not be able to attend the walk."

Come ON. My frayed emotions got the better of me. I burst into tears.

I'd raised those funds because I cared about those fighting a tough disease. I also really wanted that moment captured. An amazing highlight near the end of a craptastic year.

Sidebar to Matt Bomer: Thank you again for the signed event poster. And if you're reading this and ever find yourself in Wisconsin, let's make that photo happen.

I considered skipping the walk altogether. I was exhausted from my birthday "celebration" the day before and had already raised the money. But I owed it to my donors to attend.

I drove to Milwaukee by myself. I definitely didn't want my husband's company. On the way home, I stopped by my dear friend Kate's house. She listened, gave me the biggest hug, some cake, and yet another birthday greeting featuring Matt Bomer. Great minds think alike.

For the next few weeks, I activated total bitch mode. If my husband messaged me, I replied with a one-word answer. I know, immature. But a grown-ass woman was allowed to be immature sometimes.

As it turned out, he *had* planned a birthday celebration for me. He'd talked to the owner of FIVE and started an invitation on social media. But two months before my birthday, the kids' dad changed our custody schedule, derailing the party.

And? I still didn't understand. Why didn't he change the date? I brought it up.

He instantly went on the defensive. "Aren't you someone who believes it's the thought that counts?"

I felt like garbage and cried myself to sleep. Again.

The vicious cycle continued. He tried. He wanted to do something. I told myself I shouldn't be so hard on him. I should be happy that he'd had the idea.

My sister disagreed because he hadn't followed through. It was as if he wanted credit for waking up and getting dressed but not actually going into work. I imagined him sitting on the couch in a suit and tie. I'd scrunch up my face, and he'd whine, "I got dressed though!"

Speaking of getting dressed, I've been obsessed with fashion shows for decades. In middle school, my school put on a fundraiser with students as the models. I knew I'd arrived when I rocked the runway in a pair of Guess! jeans.

Every October, social media reminded me about an annual local fashion show that supported domestic violence survivors. Year after year, I missed the event. For one reason or another, it never worked out. But it was past time to rewrite that story. When the alert popped up, I checked my calendar. I had no plans. My husband needed to work that night. Fine by me. I asked a few friends to join me. No dice. So, I put on a super cute dress, my wig, a fabulous hat, and went alone. I mingled. I happily accepted compliments. I made new friends.

Life goes on.

At home, time dragged. My husband and I communicated but only about logistics—groceries, kids, work schedules. We watched our TV shows together, but I sat on the opposite end of the couch. Anything more than that spiraled into yelling (him) and crying (me). We needed help.

"You and I talking to each other isn't working," I told him. "I think we should see a therapist."

"Okay, we can do that," he agreed.

"Can you take the lead on setting up an appointment?" I asked.

"Yeah, I can call from work," he said.

I sent him a list of providers. I only had to remind him a few times before he scheduled an appointment. I took that as a sign of hope.

The end of the month gifted us with some time apart. The husband drove to Minneapolis to compete in a barbershop choir competition. I scored a cheap flight to Austin to celebrate my favorite holiday with KG. I needed an amazing Halloween costume. Did I own my baby chick persona or pop on a wig? I typed "bald female characters" into the search bar. GI Jane? Nah. Sigourney Weaver from *Alien*? Pass. Anne Hathaway from *Les Misérables*? Too depressing. Then came a stroke of genius! Eleven. Yes, the badass from *Stranger Things*. That human was my kindred spirit.

I completely owned that look. My best friend surprised me with the dress. I gave myself dark circles under my eyes and put red lipstick under my nose. More than one partygoer thought I actually had a nosebleed that night. My best friend promised me an amazing weekend.

And to quote the incomparable Eleven, "Friends don't lie."

BLOCKED AND DELETED

The following weekend marked high school musical time. No, not *High School Musical* with Baby Zac Efron. Local high school musicals. I was connected to many teens in theater. When you bond with someone on stage in one show, you sit in the audience for their next. I wasn't excited to sit next to my husband in the performing arts center, but I refused to skip the show. I put on my best face for my young friends. They did not deserve to deal with our marital problems.

The car ride home was quiet and awkward. When it was over, my husband retreated to the basement. Not because of my anger. Because he snored like a freight train and wanted me to be well rested. He'd been sleeping down there for months. I gave him credit for trying.

I ended up not getting a minute of rest that night. He gets credit for that too. First, a stranger messaged me on social media. *Your husband is a real slime ball.* Then another person commented on an old picture of me and my husband in Central Park. *If you only knew what your husband was up to.* We were on our honeymoon, which made it that much creepier. But it was the words written by a female that really got to me. *Your husband tried to cheat on you with me.*

Umm. Sorry. What? What did I just read?

My first thought was to blow it off. Because nope. Not possible. Delete and block all of them. Move on and go to sleep.

But then I started to heat up like I had an internal oven. Three different people in one night? My heart raced. What were the odds?

I couldn't ignore all three of them. Wondering would drive me crazy. So, I replied to the girl. The back-and-forth messages continued for at least a couple hours. The way she talked about my husband? She knew him. The racing in my heart escalated into a full-out sprint.

Needing to know if this was real, I asked for screenshots multiple times. If she was from his past, fine by me. But if not . . .

And she was not.

She finally relented and sent some screenshots. I zoomed in on his profile image. And was met by an immediate punch to the gut. Sure enough, it was his account. The picture was current. How did I know? His shirt repped my job—an organization he hadn't known about before he met me.

Excuse me while I go throw up.

Having to be sure, without a shadow of a doubt, I read the messages. They sounded like him. More precisely, the tone of the conversation reminded me of when he and I had first messaged each other. I even recognized his frequent typos from our current texts. His bumbling fingers gave him away. For the first time in months, I forgot about my cancer in one hell of a *Silver Linings Playbook* moment.

My mind reeled, my thoughts spinning every which way. He was sexting with another woman. How could he do that to me? Especially while I was fighting for my life. And why was I only finding this out now? I later discovered this woman had been baiting my husband into sexual conversations and then blackmailing him to get back at one of their mutual friends.

Too many screenshots later, I stopped messaging her. I wanted to sleep. Ha! As if. I read a book for a couple hours. Then I started texting friends.

My friend Pei-Pei responded first. I was never more grateful for her hockey-playing son. If she hadn't had to get up and drive him to a game, there was no way in hell she'd be awake at 4 a.m.

My sister texted a bit later, and I shared the first two screenshots with her.

Her response? *WOAH. WOAH. WOAH.* Omg. Need more info. *OH MY GOD. OH. MY. GOD.* Jaimie. I'm so sorry.

Somehow after that, I fell asleep. Head pounding, I woke up not enough hours later. Luckily, my husband had already left for work early.

An hour later, my phone chimed to tell me he'd posted on social media. Interesting, because he didn't post very often. *If anyone sees any weird messages about me, I've been hacked. I take special care to keep my account secure and feel violated.*

Hacked? What a load of crap. How stupid did he think I was?

That evening, he hosted a game night with friends, and I had a moms' night in at my close friend Heather's house. To this day, I'm so grateful that those plans were already made. My friends listened in disgust, and I made the wise decision to sleep at Heather's house.

The next morning, I cycled through my options. Did I confront him with the screenshots? Even if I did, would he tell me the truth? Did I take my cue from him and wait for it to play out? That evening, I sat huddled in the living room waiting for him to come home, almost in shock, knees pulled up to my chest.

He walked into the room in the most casual way. "So, has anyone reached out to you?"

Could he be more of a coward? "Yes dear, someone has."

"She reached out to me to say hi because we have a mutual friend in common. Turns out we met at the friend's party years ago. It started out totally innocent."

Side note: Is it ever really innocent—or even okay—to chat with a stranger on social media if you choose to keep it a secret from your spouse? In case you missed it—like he did—that's a rhetorical question.

"Then it got crazy," he kept talking. "And I stopped it and blocked her."

I wanted so much to believe him that I gave him the benefit of the doubt. Stupid, I know. But I did make one thing crystal clear. "If you did this, you're that guy. The guy who cheated on his wife while she fought cancer." I held up my phone, showing him a screenshot from their tête-à-tête.

"I know." He looked me in the eye. "I did chat with her for a little bit, but I didn't say those things. She made up the rest of the conversation. I was hacked."

The next day, I had no less than five chat boxes open, blowing up my closest friends. Was it even possible for him to have been hacked that way? I had screenshots. But they were blurry. That seemed suspicious, right? And with technology, crazy things could happen.

Almost every one of my friends didn't believe him. No way. They agreed he'd cheated on me. My sister helped with the missing piece. "You need to know exactly when he blocked her. You can figure that out."

I took her advice. That evening, I asked for his phone, and he gave it to me. I looked for a time stamp. Exactly when did he stop and block Instahoe? For the record, my best friend coined the name, and I'm forever grateful.

"You can't see the messages because I blocked her," he said as I scrolled through his phone.

"Maybe if you unblock her, they'll come back."

"There's only one way to find out."

I handed him back his phone and watched him click "unblock," then took it back.

The messages quickly appeared. Turns out, he was telling the truth. Well, half of it. They conversed about a mutual friend and living in Madison. I guess I could live with that. Then, the conversation took a hard turn.

Instahoe: You want something to think about for later? Want to peek at my pussy?

"This was when you blocked her right?" I asked him. It was not.

My husband: Are you sure you want to do that?

Wow, how considerate of him.

Instahoe: So, do you not want me to?

My husband: If you want to, sure. I won't hold it against you, that's for sure.

I scrolled a tiny bit more... and BAM! Her lady parts right in my face. I almost vomited all over his phone. "Is this when you blocked her?"

After about a half hour of me interrogating him, he said sheepishly, "I wasn't hacked at all."

No shit, idiot. I already knew that. And I had nothing to say to him.

If only I could block and delete a human being in real life.

QUICK LOOK

Two days later, my husband and I drove to therapy together in dead silence. The office was ten minutes away. But it felt like an hour.

We settled on opposite ends of the couch and went through the motions. He put on a sad face and admitted how dumb his choices were.

I gritted my teeth and willed my eyes not to roll too far back into my head.

The therapist kept her game face and asked the tough question. "What do you want?"

"I don't know," was all I could muster in the moment.

"I want to stay married," my husband croaked.

"What can he do to regain your trust?" the therapist directed to me.

"I don't think there's anything he can do." I knew right then and there that our marriage was over.

Nevertheless, I proceeded to torture myself for months. During that time, I went to therapy alone, read books about marriage and forgiveness, and drove myself crazy. I bawled every single day. How could he do this to me?

In case you're wondering, I asked him that very question one night. And he said, "I didn't think you'd ever find out."

Wow. Integrity much? That was the kind of person I'd married? Someone who was fine with doing something terrible as long as he didn't get caught? I went back and forth, asking myself if I really wanted to end my marriage or not. I mean, it could've been worse. He could've actually slept with her. As if virtual sex wasn't bad enough. Insert sarcasm here.

Then I remembered two things. Hilarious choice of words because I'm going to talk about breasts now. As I'd scrolled through their messages, he'd mentioned her breasts multiple times, messaging her that, "They look like fun." He told her what he would do to them. He asked her how she liked them played with.

Knife. In. My. Chest. Wall.

I had my breasts chopped off to save my life. To potentially have a future—with him. And now I was reading about him fawning over hers?

I also couldn't believe his honesty with her. Early in their messages, they'd talked about their past relationships. Then she'd asked him the million-dollar question. "Are you single?" She'd given him an out. A chance to snap out of it. To say to himself, *FUCK! I'm not single! What the hell am I doing?*

I can't say how I would've reacted if that had been his answer. Or where I would be today. But that's not what he said. He said, "Actually no, I remarried. So, you and I talking, probably not something I want known."

What a piece of trash! He chose to keep messaging her. Even though he knew it would hurt me. As I'd scrolled through their conversation, I noticed he'd been courteous enough to ignore her for a whole twenty minutes while we'd chosen the cabinets and countertops for our kitchen remodel. A true gentleman.

I also thought about something else. If I refused to stay friends with people who hurt me on purpose, why would I stay married to someone who did? And why would I put myself through this situation again?

Yes, this was familiar territory for us. A few months into my relationship with him, my boss scheduled me for a work trip. What a sweet boyfriend he was to drive me to the airport, give me a kiss goodbye, and tell me how much he'd miss me.

Three days later, when I got home, my friend Luke asked if I could talk on the phone. Not typical for us, so I agreed. He wanted to tell me about his friend Cora. A week earlier, she'd matched with my boyfriend on a dating app. The two of them had messaged on the dating app all day every day, and he'd set up a coffee date with her while I was gone. But he must've felt guilty because he canceled the date and deleted his account. Luke told me that Cora was hurt and confused, rightfully so. She had no idea my boyfriend was already in a relationship.

And I had no idea he was still dating other people. I was gutted. While we'd only been together a few months, I'd fallen in love with him. We were planning to spend our future together. In retrospect, I'm so glad he picked Cora to message. Of all the women in the greater Madison area, he'd chosen someone whose daughters regularly hung out with Luke's daughter. Otherwise, I never would've found out.

The night after I did, I asked my boyfriend point blank, "Who's Cora?"

All he said was, "Someone I've been communicating with."

Really? Like a middle-school pen pal? Cute! Not. Getting answers out of him sometimes felt like pulling teeth. He'd told me that he'd deleted all his dating apps before we'd even met. So why had he been on one?

Cause he'd gotten sucked in by a freaking marketing email—if you can believe that. I can totally picture it. An email pops up in his inbox with the subject line, We've missed you! And he says, "Yep, I have a great girlfriend right now. But might as well take a look around and see who's still out there," then clicks it open.

It didn't make sense. My brain and voice stopped working. He cried, and I held him. Like he deserved comforting. Wanting a partner without reservations, I thought about ending our relationship but quickly talked myself out of it.

He hadn't actually met with her, right? He'd broken the date. Wow. Boyfriend of the year.

INFLUENCER!

During my cancer journey, social media served as my safe space. I felt 100% comfortable sharing there. I talked about the highs, the lows, and what I'd learned along the way. Well, I never shared about the husband. That conversation only happened in person or in my closest friends' chat boxes.

What truly surprised me was how many people cared about what I had to say. The day I announced my diagnosis, I about broke the internet. Hundreds of people sent well wishes and offered to pray for me. I felt like an internet celebrity. Ha! After my last chemotherapy appointment, I posted this:

Warning: long post ahead. At least for now, today is my last chemotherapy treatment. A few months ago, this would be such a big deal. Don't get me wrong, I'm grateful to have reached this point. And to have tolerated my treatments as well as I have. But it's also anticlimactic. Herceptin is not a chemotherapy drug, but it will be given through my port every 3 weeks for another 10 months.

2018 has thrown me more curveballs and grenades than I would have liked in an entire lifetime. Even with all of this, there is good. Let me be CRYSTAL CLEAR: I don't want anyone else to get the phone call saying, "You have cancer." That unequivocally sucks. But cancer seems to give you permission for awesome things. Most importantly, to REALLY take care of yourself. I wish *that* for all the *people I love. Here are some recommendations. Permission granted. No cancer diagnosis needed.*

— Be good to yourself. Whatever that means for you.

— Figure out what you need in life and share it with the people you love.

— Know that it's okay to have high standards for yourself and the people in your life.

— Be kind and friendly to everyone. At the same time, it's okay to choose your "inner circle" very carefully. Really invest your time with them (if you want tips on choosing an inner circle, reach out. Mine is THE greatest).

If you've made it this far in reading (congratulations!!), THANK YOU for being by my side during this journey. I love you. To quote the fabulous Sara Bareilles, "You do you, Sweets."

I couldn't keep up with the reactions and comments. Love and support oozed from my computer screen. Was that how influencers felt? I was going to pretend yes—and keep posting.

RESET BUTTON

Still recovering from the Instahoe-shaped grenade tossed into my bedroom, I fell right into my own marketing trap. Diabolically placed in my inbox, Flights for $99. Even knowing the email had been created to torture me, I clicked anyway and found round-trip fare from Chicago to New York City for $125. Why the hell not? Mama needed a vacation. But could I make it work? After a mad dash to the kids' calendar told me their dad had them for the weekend, I checked off my list.

✓ First Friday without a chemotherapy treatment in 5 months
✓ Kid-free weekend
✓ Crazy cheap flight
✓ Flight booked

Now I needed a place to stay. I had friends there. No worries. I checked with Jen and Kobi first, and they couldn't host. Okay, no problem. A quick search for a hotel room killed the "cheap getaway" vibe. I started reaching out to friends to let them know I'd be in the city. Carly, who I'd worked with years ago, messaged me back first.

Carly: When are you coming?

Me: December 7-9.

Carly: Oh no, we'll be in Florida for a wedding that weekend. Where are you staying? I can give you some recommendations.

Me: I haven't figured that out quite yet.

Carly: You can have our place.

Overwhelmed, happy tears burst from my eyes. The next day, I gushed about it to my dear friend Heather.

"Can I go, too?" she asked.

"Of COURSE, you can!" I shouted.

A couple days later, she booked her flight. She'd visited twenty-five years earlier with her ex-husband but wanted to go back to see and do more. She had some unfinished business in New York City.

Reset buttons pressed for two.

PARTY PLANNER?

One evening after musical rehearsal, my daughter hurried me into the house, obviously excited about something. "You have to go downstairs."

At the bottom of the basement stairs, I turned the corner to see an adorable banner hanging on the wall. *No More Chemo!!!* My son and my friends and their families stood underneath it and shouted, "Surprise!" The husband stood off to the side.

My initial reaction was how incredibly kind. Then the questions flooded in. Was my husband trying to make up for my birthday? For our marriage? For being a grade-A jerk? While we were still living together, we didn't feel like a married couple anymore. He slept downstairs. I slept upstairs. He left for work before I got up. I barely grunted a hello when he got home. We'd stopped short at scribbling our names on the groceries in the fridge.

And if he could pull off this party, why had my birthday been beyond him? That quickly escalated to me berating myself. *What's wrong with you? You should be happy for this party. You earned it.* Wrestling with those thoughts, I tried to keep a smile plastered across my face.

I ate pizza and visited with everyone. Except my husband. I only spoke to him if he directly asked me a question. And I did so begrudgingly.

Through a few side conversations, I quickly realized that my husband hadn't had anything to do with this party. My fourteen-year-old daughter had pulled it together. She'd asked him for some help sending messages, but it was her baby—her idea to throw it and to reach out to my friends. She and her brother made the banner in my two favorite colors. Royal blue and purple. My daughter the party planner. That made a lot more sense.

MY CITY

The following Friday morning, I drove to the airport in Chicago with Heather. Giddy with excitement, my cheeks hurt from smiling so hard for three hours. Once we got settled on the plane, we talked through all our plans for the weekend. There was no time to waste once we arrived.

First things first, we needed to drop off our luggage. We navigated three train rides and a few short blocks to Carly's apartment. As promised, her keys were waiting at the front desk. My heart melted as soon as I closed the door behind me. As if a free place to stay wasn't enough, Carly had left us gifts on the dining room table. A handwritten note welcomed us to her neighborhood and offered short notes about her favorite local spots. A bottle of wine and fancy chocolate bar framed the letter. Ready to take in the city, we decided to dive into those later and rushed out the door.

On our way to the Museum of Modern Art, I called Jen to finalize our plans. Even though she and Kobi couldn't host us for the weekend, they had time for a visit.

"Does tomorrow work for you?" I asked.

She put me on speaker. "Kobi, Jaimie is up for a visit tomorrow—is morning or afternoon better?"

"How early in the morning?" I could hear his wink through the phone. "I would love to make breakfast for you."

I laughed. "Kobi, if you're willing to make breakfast for us, just tell us when and we'll be there."

We settled on ten o'clock, which gave Heather and I hours to explore the city that night. So many years since her last time there, everything was new to her. She wanted to capture our time together, and I didn't argue. She made excellent use of her new camera. Late in the evening, Heather and I posed together inside enormous LOVE block letters. Didn't that sum it all up? I felt intense love all weekend long. I enjoyed her company so much. Heather soaked up every experience, and I knew she wanted to be there with me.

As I got ready for breakfast the next morning, my phone buzzed with a text.

Jen: Would y'all be yay or nay on mimosas?

Me: YAY

An hour later, I pressed the bell for their place.

Jen wrapped me in the warmest hug as soon as I walked in.

Kobi took a break from the stove to squeeze me tight and kiss me on both cheeks.

Their daughter Glory ran to us from her bedroom, squealing in delight.

I turned around to see three filled champagne flutes on the entryway table.

"Come, sit in the oversized stuffed chair." Jen waved me and Heather into the living room.

We squooshed our bodies into it together. I sipped my mimosa and basked in the full morning sun. My heart and belly were full, thanks to Kobi serving us plate after plate full of deliciousness. In that moment, there was no place I'd rather be.

"What are you doing tonight?" As we finished eating, Jen wanted to know the rest of our plans.

"Not sure yet. Maybe a drag show?" I looked at Heather hopefully. I didn't need to twist her arm. Back when I'd attended my first drag show benefit, she'd joined me as the Joker.

"LIPS," Jen blurted out. "You have to check out LIPS." She pulled out her phone and texted me the address.

I'm so glad we took her advice. I shimmied through the busy entryway and had to catch my breath. This was not a bar but a drag palace. Jeweled chandeliers hung from a gold-plated ceiling.

Heather and I made our way to the bar. We poured over the drink menu and befriended our bartender Frankie Cocktail before the main show. My favorite number of the night? The entire cast performed "Survivor/I Will Survive." Coincidence a week after my last chemotherapy treatment? I thought not. Damn right I'd survive.

We still had to see a Broadway musical. Heather regretted not seeing one during her first visit. There were so many choices, it was tough to choose only one. We stumbled onto discount tickets for *Waitress*. I'd seen it in New York and in Madison with my husband. But I wanted a new memory associated with that show.

Message received! The universe agreed. And added a warning. Be careful what you wish for. I wept like never before in my life. I could barely see the stage it went so blurry. I needed tiny windshield wipers for my eyes.

Heather reached over and held my hand, knowing exactly what I needed in that moment.

After the show, I took her to Don't Tell Mama, my favorite piano bar in the city. "Let's make the most of our last night in the city, shall we?" I was obsessed with piano bars. They reminded me of my brother Cory. A dueling piano bar had been one of his first cleaning accounts. My brothers and sisters and I had enjoyed more than one fun night out there.

Heather loved the idea of Broadway hopefuls singing to us while serving our drinks.

I knew the piano bar wouldn't let us down. I was right.

I shed many tears on that trip and enjoyed the company of an amazing friend. I talked a lot about the future—what I wanted, what I didn't—and brunch came up. I loved brunch. Gearing up for an exhausting kitchen remodel, I made myself a promise. After months of sacrifice, the new space needed to serve a higher purpose.

Both my husband and I loved to host parties. Where did everyone gravitate? The kitchen, of course, which felt crowded with three people in it. While I wasn't excited to co-host with my husband anymore, I was sure as hell ready to do it on my own. And I couldn't think of anything better than brunch.

Post New York whirlwind, life in Wisconsin returned to normal. My husband and I continued our chilly living arrangements. I threw myself into work.

A couple weeks later, Heather stopped by. She thanked me for bringing her on the trip and handed me a card and a gift bag.

I moved the tissue paper to see the most adorable pair of slippers. Covered with a variety of cocktail glasses, they screamed brunch. I may not have figured out my marriage, but I knew how to choose the absolute best friends.

JUST A DAY IN THE PARK

Back at home, I knew only one thing.

Life goes on.

I wasn't sure about a lot of aspects of my life, but I had to get busy living. If you've watched *The Shawshank Redemption*, you know the alternative isn't so great.

Days later, I put on my silver sequin pencil skirt for a jewelry fundraising party. If I was going to help a nonprofit, I might as well get a new piece of jewelry out of the deal. I struggled with what I wanted to buy. Necklace? Earrings? I didn't know.

But I did know one thing. I didn't want my husband anymore. Before I left for the party, I finally said the words. "I don't think I want to be married to you anymore."

He simply said, "Okay."

Hold the phone. Okay? No begging or pleading? No arguing for a second chance? The fate of our marriage completely rested in my hands? Aww, hell no! Pushing that away, I walked out the door.

That night, a ring spoke to me. So bizarre, since I didn't even like wearing rings. Ever. But that one jumped off the counter straight into my heart. It reminded me of a certain princess' engagement ring. I chose a sapphire, my brother Cory's birthstone. I tried it on my left hand, then my right, where it fit perfectly. I bought that ring for myself as a tangible reminder to put myself first.

And my first step? Finish cancer treatment. My oncologist had scheduled radiation to begin at the end of December.

The day of my first session fell on the start of my husband's family's Christmas. I really didn't want to go. I could hardly stand to look at him. How could I spend the weekend with his parents, brothers, and their families and pretend everything was okay? Radiation gave me the perfect excuse not to go.

Until it got canceled. Dammit.

I drove myself and the kids separately and tried to stay away from him all weekend. I confided in my sister-in-law, and we walked outside and talked through everything. I struggled to hold it together. I may or may not have ended up listening to music and drinking alone in a random bedroom while everyone else played board games. Weirdly, I looked forward to getting back into a treatment room.

Five days a week for the next six weeks, radiation lasted twenty minutes. Driving myself to and from the appointments, I went right away in the morning. Then worked a full day afterward.

During radiation, I jammed out to music. Well, jammed out metaphorically while laying as perfectly still as possible. The radiation techs even created a new radio station for me. Vanilla Ice. Yes, I was in high school in the '90s.

Every day, I got to look at this amazing view above me. In one of the ceiling tiles, a strong, leafy tree stood against a clear blue sky on a bright sunny day. My brain took me back to Central Park. I remembered laying in the grass there a few years earlier, feeling the warmth of the September sun on my face. "I can do this," I told myself. "It's just another beautiful day in the park."

About a week in, I chatted with the tech while she prepared the room for me. "Does every room have trees?"

She smiled and shook her head. "This is the only room that has trees. The rest of them have clouds."

Cue the waterworks.

ENOUGH

I turned the calendar page to February. Still barely into the new year, I claimed it was time for a new me. While my medical team worked to heal my body, I needed to heal my heart and mind. That meant making a thoughtful, smart, and final decision about my marriage. As I read the book *Should I Stay or Should I Go*, I took notes. This quote really stood out. "Good relationships take work, but destructive relationships take everything."

Did our marriage need hard work? Or was it simply a destructive force? I read more. Journaled. Went to therapy. Often. And attended drag show therapy. Also, often. My plan for 2019 in a bulleted list was this:

- Lots of journal writing
- Alone time, resting and reflecting, allowing emotional processing to happen
- High-quality, focused time with my children
- Relaxed, enjoyable time with friends I love and trust
- Crying through sadness
- Cultivating a vision of what shape the next stage of my life would take

- Grow a new heart (Courtesy of the final chapter title in *Should I Stay or Should I Go?*)

I think back to that new year and the people who guided me toward my best self. Some of them knew every detail of my life. Others knew about my cancer but nothing else. My ex-sister-in-law checked on me regularly—something she'd been doing since the beginning of my cancer journey. While we hadn't exchanged Christmas gifts in years, she sent some major love my way.

PRO TIP: *When in doubt, gift someone a towel that says, "Don't let them treat you like free chips & salsa. You're guac, baby. Guac."*

Little did she know how much I needed to hear that. My best friend gave me a cup emblazoned with "Not today, Satan" that said everything I wanted to say on a daily basis. My daughter gave me a small dish with "I'm not a regular mom, I'm a cool mom" engraved on the bottom. Bonus points if you know what movie that quote is from.

What did my husband get me for Christmas that year?

"I was going to get you a gift card for coffee," he said. "But I didn't know if we were spending, so I didn't."

In all fairness, I wasn't expecting anything. Most years, to save money, we didn't buy each other gifts. But dude. Your marriage is hanging on by a very thin thread. If you're at all trying to make your wife feel special, try harder than a gift card—that you didn't even get around to buying!

But I made up for it and gave myself the gift of dance. I'd taken a beginning tap class when I was six. I'd been fascinated with it ever since but never took another class. Until that winter.

The first day, we all introduced ourselves. "Hi, I'm Jaimie. Excited to be here. I happen to choreograph for a local theater group and wanted more formal training."

"Which one?" the instructor asked. "I used to choreo-graph for a local group that put on modified musicals."

You've got to be kidding me. What were the chances? That one hour every Monday night brought so much joy into my life.

To stay true to my list, I spent relaxed, enjoyable time with friends. That's the only kind of time I had with my friends. They were amazing. I cooked dinner for Heather, then we danced around her kitchen. I picked up Bloom Bake Shop goodies for Liz, and we caught up on each other's lives. After Zumba one night, I met my friend Michael for dinner. Michael and I met when we'd danced with Beverly years earli-er. Easily three hours, our time together was quite relaxed. I didn't want to go home and see my husband.

And why exactly hadn't I made an official decision about my marriage yet?

One note from the book haunted me. *Could a trial separa-tion save your marriage?* I wanted to know what my life might be like without him. I needed space to process that possibility. I couldn't keep seeing him every day. But would he be willing? I finally decided to ask. "What do you think of trying a short separation?"

"If that's what you need to do," he said. "I support you in this."

My last day of radiation kicked off that trial separation. We couldn't afford for either of us to stay elsewhere for an entire week, so we made the following agreement. During the week, I worked from home and left in the evening before he got home. I returned around 10 pm, after his bedtime. He slept in the basement like before. Yes, lots of hoops. But I didn't want to see him at all for a week.

I spent that first weekend with Heather. On Friday night, we attended *Thank U, Glitz*, the first drag show at a large theater downtown. I was so thrilled for my friends to bring drag to a mainstream place. Never mind a huge venue. It was filled to capacity. The energy was electric. We had a blast.

The weekend wasn't all drag shows and brunch though. I spent a lot of time reading. And as I read, I thought about my husband so much. Given my constant anguish, I found the title of Sarah Knight's book very intriguing. If there was anyone who should *Calm the F*ck Down* . . .

Unfortunately, I wasn't calming down. At least not yet. As I read, there were so many what-ifs running around in my head. What if . . .

- He really is a great guy who made a few mistakes?
- I can't find anyone who will meet all my crazy expectations?
- I end up alone?
- *I'm* the problem?
- I say we're done and end up regretting it?

My brain ached with indecision and anxiety. A little retail therapy rescued me. Heather had a specific task at a used clothing shop, and I tagged along.

Bored, I flipped through clothes on the rack. I found an adorable summer dress and decided to try it on.

Great color on me? Check.

Fabric soft like a baby's cheek? Check.

Fun style? Check.

V so low you could see my old-lady, mom bra? Um . . . uncheck.

SIDEBAR: That is what I called the undergarment that held my prosthetics.

I meant no shade toward the manufacturer. It absolutely served a purpose. I was grateful for the prosthetics. I'd worn them for eight months post-surgery, and they'd helped me tremendously as I eased back into my "normal" life. But at the end of the day, the dress didn't work with the prosthetics.

The rest of that week, I spent my weeknights with amazing girlfriends. Friends who listened while you blabbered on for hours about your marriage. Who told you they were on your side no matter what. Who cooked you dinner and spoiled you with dessert. Who made sure to save a mug for you when it was time for boozy hot cocoa. A mug with "You are ENOUGH" printed in bold black letters.

And you, dear reader. Please know that you are enough too.

HILLS

The week apart gave me the gift of clarity. Vision. A picture of my life without my husband in it. A pretty great life, actually. No matter what, I needed to choose me.

And, of course, the very next week he and I were scheduled to go on a trip together. His first half marathon in Austin, Texas. Fantastic timing. Yes, that was the sound of my eyes rolling all the way back into my head.

Long before my diagnosis, we'd registered together for a race in San Francisco to honor my friend Sarah, who was fighting AML. We'd started fundraising for that half marathon in plenty of time. But after my diagnosis, plans changed. I realized I would be in my third month of chemotherapy on race weekend. So, we'd signed up for a different race in Austin the following February.

That summer, in the thick of treatment, two of my friends created a fundraising team in my honor. I was humbled. Unfortunately, treatment derailed my resolve to train. At the peak of my training season, I logged only four miles. I didn't want to run more than that. But I'd completed a half marathon before. Without a doubt, I could do it again.

Important disclaimer: I do not recommend this training plan.

Fast forward to February. I had a promise to keep. A half marathon to run.

My daughter asked, "Can we come cheer?"

"Absolutely," I told her.

My incredible support team of friends and family had rallied and raised over $100,000 and earned the privilege of linking my brother Cory's name with cutting-edge research. My dad, a two-time blood cancer survivor, joined us for the weekend.

My head and heart hurt all weekend. But the ground-breaking work of finding a cure for cancer deserved all the attention, so I pretended to be fine. Especially in front of my kids and my dad. But he knew. Too smart for his own good, that guy. Still, I managed to sidestep his concern.

I did my best to soak up the joy in that weekend. KG hosted us at her house and continued to be my rock. Our first day, the thermometer soared past 80 degrees. A hot sunny day in mid-February. We walked to the park, and my tweens chased her giggly toddler. In other important news, my son tried queso for the first time. If he could fly a plane, he'd go back to Austin just for that.

The night before the race, KG showed me the shirts she'd made for the kids and her family to wear while they cheered. I was grateful I saw them in advance. The race challenged me plenty. I did not need to approach mile six and see my army of cheerleaders with shirts that read:

My Friend
My Daughter
My Mom

My Boo

My Queen

My favorite part of any marathon weekend? The specta-tors' posters. They're truly an art form. Highlights from that day?

YAASSS KWEEN

Hills are like breakups u gotta get over them

YASS Jaimie (created by my co-workers, complete with a pic of me and my current faux hawk)

The downside from that day? Close proximity to my hus-band. He made my skin crawl. So how could we run 13.1 miles side by side? I encouraged him to run on his own. He outpaced me. It made sense, regardless of the state of our marriage.

He heard nothing of it. "No, we planned to run this to-gether, and that's what I'm going to do!"

Welp. We also planned for you to be faithful and to not sext a complete stranger. And look what happened there. But I sucked it up. I didn't want to make a scene. Or make the weekend more difficult for anyone else. Did he run the en-tire half marathon by my side? Yes. Was that the experience I was hoping for when we originally signed up? Not even close. While all half marathons include the same mileage, it felt like the longest race of my life.

Afterward KG hosted a victory party at her house. Other longtime friends joined in the fun. I steered clear of my hus-band and enjoyed myself.

The next morning, I sat in the airport and posted about the weekend on social media. I thanked KG's mom for mak-ing cookies for us. I highlighted my dad's speech the night before the race. I explained my reason for doing the event and why I was grateful for every single donation.

I failed to mention my husband. On purpose.

I couldn't talk about him and be honest. And I couldn't be a hypocrite and lie to my friends. Eleven would be so disappointed in me. Needing some distance from his reactions and comments, I wrote the post and blocked him from being able to see it.

Late that evening, back at home, he exploded. "I saw your post. Did it mean nothing to you that I ran thirteen miles next to you? You brought up the *cookies* but didn't mention me?"

As he yelled at me for not stroking his ego on social media, I realized that I could single-handedly save our marriage—if I did all the work. If I made sure he felt good all the time. If I never chose me. But what kind of marriage was that?

Not-so-subtle hint: Maybe that wasn't the kind of marriage for me.

RUBY

On the first day of the kitchen remodel, I felt generous. Ever so thoughtful, I texted the husband the before photos. It was his house too.

Husband: Are you excited for this?!

Me: Yes and no. Are you?

Husband: Excited for completion and the change. It's going to be a mess, though.

Memories betrayed me. We'd picked out the final pieces for the kitchen in between his messages to Instahoe. And that obviously didn't even cross his mind.

A couple weeks later, I started reading a book about focusing on what sparks joy in your life. If something doesn't spark joy for you, you get rid of it. I stumbled across a meme about the book. A woman stood in the doorway behind the outline of a man walking away, suitcase in hand.

Narrator: Does it bring you joy?

Me: Throws husband out.

Let me tell you, I cackled.

All joking aside, I still hesitated to end my marriage. Did I really want to start over? Enter Glinda and my often-prophetic, page-a-day calendar. "You've always had the power, my dear, you just had to learn it for yourself."

Fine, witch. Heard you loud and clear. Now give me my ruby red slippers.

Sure enough, I clicked my heels three times and transported to FIVE. Where there was fun, love, support, and glitter for good measure.

There really was no place like home.

CLAPS

The kitchen remodel turned out to be extensive. My bedroom and the kitchen completely traded places. While the house was being torn up, we put the stove in the garage and squeezed the refrigerator into the living room. My mattress and box spring ended up in my son's room. For a couple months, while my husband slept in his usual room in the basement, I slept in my "new bedroom" on a futon next to said refrigerator and a small rolling cart with a microwave and crockpot. My back ached. My head throbbed. Exhaustion ruled my days and nights.

Since my husband and I rarely spoke, I looked forward even more to spending time out with friends at FIVE. I arrived one night to see Ricky on the customer side of the bar for a change. While I enjoyed his bartending skills, I was excited to sit and visit with him.

"How have you been?" he asked.

No longer willing to make excuses for my husband's behavior, I offered an earful—marriage struggles, my birthday, and finally Instahoe.

Ricky yelped in surprise. "Oh. FUCK that ho!" He enunciated each word again, with a clap.

"FUCK" (clap)

"THAT" (clap)

"HO!" (clap)

That helped me cope for months. Not that I encouraged swearing across the board, but if someone does you that wrong, it is kind of therapeutic to yell, "Ohhhh, fuck that ho!"

You're welcome.

Keep reading for more life tips.

SCARS

That spring, I made up my mind. I was no longer going to be a wife. While the romantic relationship ended with my husband, my living situation stayed the same. We'd committed to the remodel. I wanted to stay in the house no matter what, and I couldn't afford to do that by myself. So, my husband became my housemate. My stomach churned whenever he entered the room.

Then he opened his mouth. "How's your day?"

Eye roll. It was better ten seconds ago.

"Do we need more milk?"

Umm, did you think to look in the fridge?

Annoyed and irritated all the time, I pledged to heal myself. I attended therapy with the focus of a C+ high-school student determined to make the honor roll. I focused on my friends and my kids. I knocked the possibility of romance right off the table. That spring, I went to more drag shows a week than ever before. And in each short drive over, I sobbed. Then I shut off the car, wiped my eyes, and told myself, "You can't cry at a drag show."

FIVE felt safe. Loving. Friends hugged and kissed me and told me I looked fabulous. I didn't feel fabulous with my peach fuzz head. But damn, I felt like I was on fire with my wig on. I remembered watching a TV show with a breast cancer survivor ripping off her wig in the middle of her speech at a big fundraiser. So relatable.

As if my dumpster fire of a living situation wasn't enough, my skin started to feel as if it was actually on fire. I'd survived six weeks of radiation with minimal side effects. At my last appointment with the radiation oncologist, I was hopeful. "Does this mean I won't have any issues at all?"

"Oh no, you'll feel something. Sometimes, patients feel the burn after treatment stops," she explained.

Sure enough, ten days later my skin got red and blistered. It burned hotter than after my most intense Hawaiian sunburn. I wore a gigantic T-shirt and slathered on aloe repeatedly throughout the day.

One day, I needed something from the store. I thought about putting on my prosthetics and real clothes for a few seconds. Decided to pass. Entirely too much work. And pain.

I walked around the store, and nobody seemed to notice I was flat as a pancake. Or maybe they didn't care. Interesting. Did that mean I had a choice when it came to those hot and heavy prosthetics? Really, how many women would choose to wear a bra if they had no reason to? Be honest. I wouldn't. So, what if I just wore clothes?

I stepped into the possibility and into a new frustration. I didn't like how most of my clothes fit. V-necks were too low. Without breasts to prop up the V, the fabric draped to the middle of my stomach. Form-fitting tops gave away that I wasn't truly flat. My scars were actually indents on my chest wall. Also not a look I wanted to highlight. While I wasn't ashamed of my scars, I didn't want to display them for all to see. They were part of my story to tell, and I got to choose who heard that story. An earned privilege for those close to me.

I systematically annihilated my closet. Each piece that didn't flatter my new body went into a bag. Several bags later, my daughter and I went thrift shopping. It took stacks of clothes and hours in the dressing room, but I found a few items that worked.

Or should I say, werked?

I got excited every time I found something. But it took so much effort. Why wasn't there a clothing line specifically for people like me? I couldn't possibly be the only survivor wrestling with post-surgery fashion.

The more I thought about it, the more I wondered if I could actually launch a clothing line. I didn't know how to sew. Or design clothes. So what? Being completely unqualified hadn't stopped others before me. And honestly, I cried too much about my marriage ending. I needed somewhere else to focus my mental energy. But would trying to design a clothing line be a wise endeavor for me? I didn't know. It was time to ask around. I posted in a couple of closed online groups for breast cancer survivors.

Feeling curious. I often see posts of clothes that are great for "flatties" (which I super appreciate, by the way). My question: how would you feel about a clothing line specifically made for our bodies? Excited? Offended? Any other emotion?

A hundred women commented.

"So excited."

"That would be super cool."

"I've been praying for this."

The responses were positive and encouraging. And that last one got me. My idea was potentially an answered prayer. Though I didn't know how or what to do, I had to give it a shot.

At the very beginning of summer, my daughter and I made our way around the neighborhood garage sales. We both enjoyed bargain hunting. At the very last house, she found a bundle of old sewing patterns. Her sewing machine had been collecting dust, and she was excited for new projects. Each pattern cost twenty-five cents. We bought the entire stack. On the walk home, I flipped through them. One top jumped out at me. Hmmm. Could this inspire the first item in my clothing line?

Maybe Heather could help? In addition to being a dear friend and excellent travel companion, she was a talented seamstress. I'd seen the proof in years of elaborate Halloween costumes that she made for her entire family.

I gave her a call and cut to the chase. "I have a totally random question for you. Could I hire you to help me with a sewing project?"

"What kind of project?" she asked.

"I want to design clothing for other breast cancer survivors. I have a pattern I want to tweak a bit. Could you make the first prototype for me?"

"I'd love to!" she gushed. "I'll need the pattern and something similar that fits you well."

One specific tunic popped into my brain. I tossed it and the pattern into a bag and drove to her house.

Which tunic?

Oh, the one I'd been wearing the night I was sexually assaulted.

Maybe I should jump back to that night for just a second
. . .

FAMILY

One heavenly warm summer night, I drove to FIVE.

The show zipped along, ending earlier than usual. Sometimes the host wasn't up for chatter with the audience. A few
people made plans to go to another nightclub and asked me to
join them. While I appreciated the invites, my default answer
was usually no. FIVE was a few minutes from my house and
had a huge parking lot. At this other club, I had to fight for
street parking. Also, wasn't midnight late enough for me to be
out at my age?

"You gotta come," Ricky begged.

Since I didn't have to be up early the next morning, I
caved. "Why not?"

He raced out the door as I said my goodbyes.

Somehow, I beat Ricky there. I saw a couple other friends,
waved hello, and decided to go dance. I didn't need someone
to keep me company on the dance floor. Until I did.

A young lady, who seemed hellbent on living her best life,
was dancing all over the floor topless. Not something I would
have ever done, but I thought, *you do you.*

"Shake 'em if you got 'em." Yelling over the music, she came closer.

Feeling bold, I yelled back, "I don't have any!"

In the blink of an eye, she bent down and put her head up my tunic. Yes, the *inside* of my tunic. Her face landed a millimeter from my chest wall.

My jaw dropped. The rest of my body froze. Instead of music, I heard the blood rushing in my ears.

A second later, her head was out, and she pranced off into the night.

I still couldn't move. But my mind didn't have the same paralysis. It raced with rapid-fire questions.

What the fuck just happened?

Did that really happen?

Was I just sexually assaulted?

Wait.

Was it sexual? I don't have breasts.

I shuffled to the bar in a daze and stammered to one of my friends, "Uhhh, I think I was just sexually assaulted."

"What happened? Are you okay?" he asked.

I told him about the girl and about my confusion with my breastless situation.

"Oh my god. Yes, that is one hundred percent assault," my friend assured me. "I'm so sorry."

I stood with him until I calmed down enough to drive home.

Life goes on, right?

A few days later, as I sat in therapy, I thought about not mentioning it. I'd processed it enough. But it might be good for my therapist to be aware at least, so I relayed the story.

"What?" she shrieked. "I'm so sorry that happened to you."

Me too, lady. Me freaking too.

Then she went and ruined it by asking, "Were you drinking?"

Excuse me? Hold on one minute. How dare she? I explained that I had been drinking, but not an unusual amount for me. Our session time ended, and I gathered my things quickly. The more I thought about her question, the hotter my blood boiled. A mental health professional isn't supposed to blame the victim.

A couple days later, I shared my story on social media. I felt like it was my responsibility to use what happened to me to educate people.

> *Out one night recently, someone touched me without my consent in a way that really upset me. I'm not looking for sympathy. I have one request, though. If someone tells you a story like this, please, PLEASE do not ask them if they were drinking/drunk. PLEASE don't ask what they were wearing. If you feel the need to ask a question, you can ask something like: "How are you doing?" or "Is there anything I can do for you?" Because whatever they were wearing, whatever they had to drink—It's. Not. Their. Fault.*

My friends flooded me with support. Not surprising. I knew I'd probably preached to the choir. But if one person needed to hear that, it was worth it. Even if it was only in solidarity for people who've been sexually assaulted.

The next time I was at FIVE, I came in the back door and approached the owner. "Hi, how are you tonight?"

Carrying a huge pail of ice in each hand, he stopped and looked me right in the eyes. "I read about what happened to you, and I'm so sorry."

"Aww, thank you."

"If you don't mind me asking, was that here?"

"Oh, no. Nothing like that has ever happened here."

He nodded. "If anything ever does, you let me know. You're family."

Yes, I had the best family a girl could ever ask for.

AN APP FOR AN APP

Throughout the winter, my husband and I sporadically went to therapy together, where we went 'round and 'round about our relationship. Or rather, he waited for me to decide if I wanted to stay married to him or not. Sometimes we talked about future possibilities as single people. During one appointment, my husband announced he wasn't going on dating apps again. "Been there, done that."

I took him at his word. Had I not learned my lesson on that already? Yet at the end of May, I noticed something different about him. He exuded higher energy and had a spring in his step.

While I realized it was not my business, I asked him a bold question. "Did you have sex?" No need to beat around the bush.

"I don't want to answer that," he said.

And there was my answer.

We continued talking for a bit about it. We were friendly roommates, right? We should be able to have this conversation?

"How did you meet her?" I asked.

"A dating app," he answered.

Oof. A punch in the gut. An app again. He'd probably been thinking he'd had good luck on there before, so why not?

And here I'd thought he'd been fighting for our marriage. At least for a while. If he'd moved on so quickly, how much had he ever really loved me? Was it too much to ask for him to mourn the death of our relationship a tad longer? In a way, I was glad I found out. It was like we'd come full circle from four years earlier.

Strongly encouraged by our therapist to wait at least a year before pursuing romantic connections with other people, I'd had every intention of waiting it out. Now that I knew the husband hadn't, I decided to do some revenge dating of my own. Immature, I know. But at that point, I didn't care.

I'd never been on a dating app before. Hell, the last time I'd really dated, I was eighteen years old and a freshman in college. My curiosity piqued, I wanted to know what I'd been missing. Turns out not much. Check out some of the dudes' taglines.

Sup

deephotkiss

Cumm see what awaits

So clever. So subtle. Excuse me while I wretch.

In case you didn't quite get the full picture, another bright spot was the inquisitive conversation starters.

Thirsty???

Nope. Never less thirsty in my life.

Then there were the patient gentlemen. They waited until a few messages in before they asked, "What turns you on?"

Not you or this conversation. Glad we cracked the code and cleared that up.

Finally, welcome to the harassment portion of online dating. One day, during a very ordinary conversation, a new message appeared. I clicked on it . . . only to see an erect penis staring me in the face. Oh. Absolutely not.

"I'm out." App deleted.

BRUNCH AND SOME BUSINESS ON
THE SIDE

The remodel wrapped, and I prepared to spark joy in the new space.

I organized the kitchen and living room with brunches in mind. I used the extra cabinet space to fit all the fancy cocktail glasses that had been collecting dust in the basement. I bought new plates at the Dollar Tree because that was more me than Crate & Barrel ever will be. Picking the first Sunday I could, I posted on social media. Everyone who was interested was invited. Truly a brunch "for the people."

My shopping list included three cartons of juice, two extra-large bottles of vodka, fruit, bacon, and ingredients for my sister-in-law's baked French toast. What could I say? My friends liked *some* breakfast with their alcohol. Brunch lasted for hours, and I loved every minute of it. At the end, I made a promise. "I'll keep hosting until you don't want to come anymore." Brunch became a monthly event.

As much as I loved that time, starting my clothing business burned in the back of my mind. I knew I had a great idea on my hands. I also knew I needed help. I called Andrea, who worked at a local business that supported women entrepreneurs. "Hi! I'm not sure if you remember me. Last year you met with my daughter and I about a dog-walking business."

"Yes, I remember," she said pleasantly. "How can I help you?"

"I now have a business idea of my own. Could we sit down together to discuss it?"

"I would be happy to meet with you."

We squeezed in a meeting before my kids were home for summer vacation.

After we visited for a bit, she asked the magic question. "So, what kind of business do you want to start?"

"I'd like to create a clothing line designed specifically for breast cancer survivors."

You could hear a pin drop.

Then she said, "Mmmhh. Fashion is hard . . ."

My heart sank.

"But I believe it's viable."

My heart soared.

Very well then! Onward and upward. Hadn't I been doing "hard" for a good year or so already? I could do something hard for a good reason now.

That very night, I met my friend Tempestt for dinner. We'd never spent time together outside of FIVE before, but I followed her on social media and felt like she was inside my head. She seemed to have a singular mission in life: support every person she could to be the very best version of themselves and know their worth. I needed to get to know her better. To spend more time in her space.

Over dinner, we talked about so much—plans for the future, relationships, dreams. Still excited about my meeting that morning, I shared my clothing idea with her. Over and over, she kept saying how important it was for me to try. She was building up her business as a DJ in town as well, which exploded over time.

As summer flew by, I wasn't ready to share yet with the online world, but I also couldn't keep it a secret when friends asked me what was new. I told them about my business idea, and they were all incredibly kind and positive.

My favorite reaction came from Kate, who said, "I think it's the most amazing idea I've heard in a long time. And you're going to do it right and end up being super rich and famous. Then you just, BOOM, kick hubby to the curb. Pack yo shit, Loser."

PRO TIP: *Get yourself friends who respond like that.*

After a drag show one night, I felt inspired to share my idea with Kayos, one of the first queens I met as a pageant show backup dancer.

Tears welled in her eyes, and she took my cheeks in her hands. "That's amazing."

The next day, Andrea called me. "Jaimie, I want to help you, but I don't have much experience in apparel."

"I understand."

"You should talk to Jill. She works in the business department at a local college. She also helps small businesses get started."

"I'd love to connect with her. Thanks so much for thinking of me."

Within minutes, an email popped up in my inbox. Andrea addressed it to me and Jill. "I'm writing to find out if you have any suggestions or connections to people in the apparel industry?"

Jill replied and introduced me to her colleague Betty, the director of their Fashion Merchandise Program. Eager to learn from both of them, I knew I had plenty to discover about entrepreneurship and the fashion industry.

On the first day of July, I drove to campus to meet Jill. The sun beat down on me as I walked from the parking lot and into Jill's office. Opening up my most professional business portfolio, I waited for wisdom, and she delivered.

Jill suggested I enroll in the Entrepreneurial Training Program (ETP) offered through the Small Business Development Center at UW-Madison. A proud Badger, I was excited about the possibility of being on campus again. I left Jill's office and nearly floated to my car.

I got home to see a new message from Jill introducing me to her ETP contact. "I had the privilege of meeting with Jaimie today, and I wanted to connect the two of you. Jaimie is looking at starting a clothing/apparel line for those who either choose to not have reconstructive surgery after a mastectomy or cannot have reconstructive surgery for whatever reason. She is applying to your ETP course and has already researched many options and resources. I will let you both take it from here. Thank you!"

Spoiler alert: I was accepted into the program. Fist bump.

The following day, I drove back to campus to meet Betty. The *clack* of my heels announcing my arrival, I strode into the main café area.

Betty looked up from her book and smiled at me.

I shook her hand, sat down, and opened my notebook, ready to scribble furiously.

"I understand you want to start a clothing line. What do you want to know?" she asked.

"Everything," I replied with an eager smile. "I have a prototype in the works."

"Wonderful. Are you sewing it?"

"Ummm . . ." I fidgeted. "I don't know how to sew."

"That's okay." She smiled again. "A great next step is to find a designer. You should talk to Lindsay. She teaches a class on design here and runs a resale shop in town."

"Upshift Lindsay? I know her already. I've been shopping there for years."

Mental note: I had something new to talk about with Lindsay next time I saw her.

Jill, Betty, and Andrea each taught me something new and different when I met with them. But they all echoed each other in giving me one piece of advice: you need to write a business plan.

Andrea checked in with me regularly. Every meeting, email, and call ended the same way. "Let me know if there is anything I can do to help your business." I kept asking questions and letting her help me.

We sat down together at Lane's Bakery, pouring through the first draft of my business plan. I mean, why not enjoy a chocolate frosted donut while planning to launch a clothing line? It was clear to both of us that I needed to know more about apparel.

"I'm going to talk to some of our other teammates who may know more details on apparel," Andrea offered.

"That would be wonderful. I'd really appreciate that."

"I did find an article about Lev Apparel. They focus on helping women. Those who wear the apparel, and the artisans who make them. Maybe they can help."

"It can't hurt to ask." I set down my donut. "I feel like I'm spinning my wheels and not really accomplishing anything."

"You're going through a lot." She shook her head. "Give yourself a break and some time to work this business. It's okay. Rome was not built in a day."

"You're so right." And she was. I had a lot on my plate. "Thanks for the reminder."

We said our goodbyes, and I raced back home to emails from my full-time job.

That evening, I clicked on the link Andrea shared about Lev Apparel. I loved reading about what they did. Thinking what the hell, I filled out the contact form on their site. "Hello Krystle, I learned about you from Andrea. I am planning to launch a niche apparel line, and I'd very much like to connect. Best, Jaimie."

She responded by mid-morning. "Hey Jaimie, thank you for reaching out. How exciting! Abby and I would love to connect with you. Would you mind sending out some dates that would work? Looking forward to it!"

I met with them in their office space downtown. I loved their energy the second I walked in the door. They were warm, welcoming, and supportive. They asked me about why I wanted to create this line and shared more of their own backstory. The openness was refreshing. With every question they asked, I learned more.

"What's your next step?" Krystle asked.

"I'm trying to find a designer."

They looked at each other and said, almost in unison, "You could be the designer."

"Oh!" I laughed. "Even though I can barely sew a button?"

"Absolutely. You know what works. Think of what you want to create. You can start with an existing piece you'd like to modify. Take all of that to a patternmaker."

I scribbled more notes and thanked them profusely for their time.

"Keep going," Krystle said. "You're doing women a service!"

I left with hope in my heart. Both for the possibility of my line, and in gratitude for women supporting each other.

The next day, I emailed Lindsay. I couldn't wait for my next shopping trip. "Since I last spoke with Betty, I am moving in a different direction. I was looking for a designer. Now I am contemplating working with a patternmaker rather than a designer. Could one of your students potentially fill that role?"

Two days later, Nancy appeared in my inbox. "Lindsay gave me your contact information. I am interested in helping you for the breast cancer cause."

What was that about women supporting women?

Nancy and I met for the first time at a local library. She was pleasant, kind, and cared very deeply about helping breast cancer survivors. It couldn't have been a better connection.

While I still had so much to learn and do before launching my clothing line, I felt bolstered by every person who supported me along the way. When I got frustrated and thought about scrapping the whole idea, I heard their words in my head. I believed in the idea, but damn, it didn't hurt to have fabulous people in my corner.

VICTOR/VICTORIA

Many years ago, when I was married to my first husband, I fell in love with a girl named Serena. Serena van der Woodsen.

Okay, I fell in love with Blake Lively from *Gossip Girl*. Whatever. Minor detail. At the time, I assumed everyone was in love with her. Look at her, for crying out loud. In the far depths of my mind, I wondered if I was attracted to women. Even if I was, what would I do about it? If you were raised Catholic, you didn't end a marriage because you might be attracted to someone else.

Fast forward to this summer and a social media event suggestion. "We think you would like to attend the Lesbian Pop-up Bar." Color me intrigued. Madison didn't have an official lesbian bar, so an organizer had created the event to take over a specific bar for the evening. It happened once a month, but I was never free when they popped up. As an ally, I proudly wore a shirt declaring, *Love is Love* with Wonder Woman and Supergirl kissing each other. I didn't need to be a card-carrying lesbian to pop into the event, right?

I drove across town and arrived at the restaurant to find no signage. What was I supposed to do? Walk up to a table and ask, "Hey, are you the lesbians?"

I walked up to the bar instead and found an old friend bartending. We hadn't seen each other in years, not since our sons were in elementary school together. After the usual quick pleasantries, not in the mood to make small talk, I scurried off to the bathroom where I texted his ex-wife.

Me: Uhhh. Is your ex bartending tonight by any chance?

Kelly: Lol yep. R u there?

Me: Yep.

Kelly: Haha. With who?

Me: Soooooooo weird. Especially since I decided to show up for the lesbian pop-up bar tonight.

Kelly: Bahahahahaha. That's amazing.

Having driven a half hour to be there, I wasn't going to give up so easily. But I needed time to figure out what I was going to do. I left the bathroom and returned to my friend at the bar.

"Who are you meeting here?" he asked me.

Here went nothing. "Do you know where the lesbian pop-up bar is?"

Bless his heart, he must have been so confused. Last he knew, I was definitely married to a man. But he didn't bat an eye when he pointed behind me. "I think it's that table over there."

He was right, and I met a fabulous group of ladies. Victoria really intrigued me. She wore a vintage dress and hairstyle and a beautiful smile.

As the conversations died down, I was ready to head home. I thanked everyone at the table for a lovely evening and stopped by the bar to say goodbye to my friend.

Victoria came up to pay her bill, and we walked out together. Before we got to our cars, I asked for her phone number. Not having dated since college, was that even how it worked now? I guessed so. She gave it to me.

The next day, I flew out of town for a work conference. Being a high extrovert and working from home the last six years was an interesting combination. I'd become close with several colleagues, and time with them in real life was a dream. Our last conference like this had been two weeks after my second wedding.

It was very surreal to be with my coworkers again with my marriage being over. Some knew. Many didn't. There wasn't really an appropriate social media post like #divorced #sextinghappens, so I told colleagues in person. But only if they asked about my personal life. It was actually freeing to tell my former boss, who still sat in our weekly virtual staff meetings.

As I embarked on a new chapter in my life, the signs in our conference room tugged at my heart. It was as if they were directives written specifically to challenge me.

Be Genuine

Be Remarkable

Be Worth Connecting With

I vowed to be all of those as I watched the rain on my way to the airport. As I looked out the plane window, a rainbow was ready to take me home. I took it as a sign. The next day I texted Victoria.

Me: Hi Victoria! Hope you've been well. Any chance you'd like to get coffee together sometime?

Victoria: Been doing great. How's it going for you? I would love to go for coffee.

The following Saturday was date day. I'd been on how many dates and been married twice, yet I was still so nervous. But it was a giddy, excited nervous.

We sat together at an outside table in the sunshine and spoke for hours. She smiled as she spoke, and my body relaxed completely. We had so much in common, including having teenagers very close in age. I mentioned my drag show plans for that night.

"I love drag," she said.

The next day, I asked if she'd like to join me at a drag show that week. Done and done. Dating a woman was easy. I got to the bar early that night and found Rob, one of my favorite bartenders.

"How are you tonight, honey?" he asked with a smile.

"I have a date tonight." I was sure I was grinning from ear to ear.

"Okay, what's he like?" Rob wanted details.

"*Her* name is Victoria," I said.

"Oooohhh." Rob's eyes twinkled. "I'll keep an eye out for her!"

Victoria waltzed in wearing a vintage polka-dot dress. Swoon. We sat close together, whispering in each other's ears at different points during the show. I could work with this. After the show, I walked her to her car. I thought about kissing her but chickened out. We hugged instead.

I went back inside and marched up to Rob. "So, what did you think?"

"She is gorgeous."

Over the next couple weeks, Victoria and I texted back and forth a bit. We were getting very close to Pride Weekend, which we'd talked about on our coffee date. I thought maybe we could go together but didn't want to be too presumptuous. I texted her to test the waters.

Me: Hi! Still looking forward to Pride Weekend?

She didn't answer. At all. If texts had busy signals, that's what I would've heard. Beep. Beep. Beep. And I never heard from her again.

Maybe dating a woman wasn't so easy after all.

ABOVE AND BEYOND

That same month, my husband and I made a big decision. He'd move out, and I'd stay in the house. I was the one with two teenagers left to raise.

I was beyond ready to not be housemates anymore, but I needed help to pay the mortgage. We'd picked that house with both our salaries in mind. Luckily, I lived in a college town, my house was adorable, and the basement was renter ready. I posted on multiple places online. Piece of cake. Well, less cake and more of an oatmeal raisin cookie . . . when you asked for chocolate chip. Because I got nothing.

As the temperature rose, so did my stress. If I couldn't find a renter, how exactly was I going to pay my mortgage? I was more than a couple bucks short. Could I sell my house? Quite possibly. And live where exactly? I didn't have anything against living in an apartment, but when rent was the same as a mortgage payment, what was the point?

I got creative and decided to book guests for the downstairs bedroom. My first guest—Finn from Boston—booked a five-day stay. His profile picture showed a good-looking guy. I wasn't complaining. We exchanged numbers so he could let me know when to expect him.

At the end of my last staff meeting before Labor Day weekend, my team each shared what we'd be doing. When it was my turn, I showed them Finn's profile picture. My colleagues should know what he looked like. He could be a serial killer. We joked about me picking him up at the airport and romance ensuing. They all had a good feeling about it. Belief in the good of humanity and all that. And one extra romantic colleague piped up with, "It's like a Nicholas Sparks novel."

The day Finn from Boston arrived, we texted back and forth. I about fainted when he said he was two minutes away. I hadn't had this much communication with a handsome, straight man in quite some time.

He rang the doorbell, and I jumped to answer it.

Cute face? Check.

Dreamy eyes? Check.

6'2" frame? Unexpected bonus.

I showed Finn his room downstairs, complete with my sweet note welcoming him into my home and a list of fun summer things to do in Madison. I'd never hosted a total stranger before, so I caught him up to speed on what to expect from me. "I'm social, but I also can amuse myself and leave you alone. If you want a dinner recommendation, I can give you one. If you want company, I haven't eaten, and there's a good place around the corner."

"Sure," he said. "I'd like company. Maybe we can go in forty-five minutes?"

I went back upstairs to relax. It was odd to not have plans on a Friday night. Other than a few drag shows, I actually didn't have any plans for the entire weekend. I guess the Universe was making plans for me.

Forty-five minutes later, Finn texted me that he was almost ready to go.

On that gorgeous August night, we walked to the neighborhood tavern, chatting like old friends catching up after years of not seeing each other. At dinner, we talked about our failed relationships and my cancer diagnosis but not what type of cancer I had.

It wasn't a date, but it sure felt like one. And I didn't mind that one little bit.

On the way home, he mentioned going downtown that night. I had a friend's dog to watch and was in for the night. But that didn't mean I couldn't do him a favor. From my comfy spot on the couch, I texted him my kind offer.

Me: If you want, I'm happy to give you a ride downtown. Then it's an Uber back.

Yes, that was me being kind. No ulterior motive.

Finn: Wow that's really nice. I'd want to give you what the ride would have cost me.

Me: No need. It's an easy drive for me down there.

I mean, dude, that kind of defeated the entire purpose of my offer. And honestly, I lived fifteen minutes from the capitol.

Finn: I'd have to repay you somehow. Laundry? Dishes? Gardening? < laughing crying emoji >

Me: < 3 laughing crying emojis > I have a few days to decide.

Finn: Yes, you do. Can be anything you want haha

Hold. The. Phone. Anything I want? Did he say what I think he said? In case you forgot, he was hot. And I'd found out a piece of new information. The guy was twenty-nine.

That gave me some numbers to review. Twenty-nine. Forty-two. Zero.

He was twenty-nine.

I was forty-two.

I had zero breasts.

I never imagined I'd be single at this age. And with those numbers, I didn't expect people to be knocking down my door. Definitely not a hot twenty-nine-year-old. I gave him a ride downtown and came back to a quiet night at home with my TV.

The next day he planned to hit the Farmers' Market and the Taste of Madison, both on my fantastic list of things to do. Once again, I asked if he wanted company. I explained how much I loved the Farmers' Market and wouldn't have many more chances to go this season. Both true statements. And off we went.

We walked around the entire capitol square, then down State Street and back. He tried cheese curds and shared them with me. It was the greatest date that wasn't a date. Fine by me.

That night I needed some drag in my life. I'd told my friends about Finn and his "it can be anything you want haha" text. Some were nervous for me, pointing out, "You have to be careful" and "He's your guest." Others didn't have the same reservations.

The next day some friends wanted to meet up at Taste of Madison. I let Finn know, and he was down for more time together.

My friends were moving like molasses, so Finn and I stopped at the park first. We walked around for a while and laid down in the grass by the lake. Days like this were why I was willing to live in Madison the rest of the year when it was subzero. Kidding. A little bit.

I finally met up with friends, and he went off on his own to explore the city. As he walked away, I let him know there was a drag show that night if he wanted to come. Turns out, he'd thought about it the night before. So much so that he had FIVE's address in his phone.

I went home to change clothes, picking something I knew looked good on me. Sadly, he didn't show, but I still had a blast with my friends. Afterward, some of them wanted to head over to the club where I'd been assaulted. I agreed because I'd be with a large group and knew at least two friends who'd be looking out for me.

Tiffany—who was still Tiffany at the time but now goes by Tristan—came over and said, "You have to meet Mathias."

She introduced us, and the three of us bantered back and forth for a bit. Mathias and I focused more on each other, and Tiffany took off for the dance floor. There was a pretty girl who needed her attention. And her lips.

Apparently, my lips also needed attention. All of a sudden, Mathias kissed me. We were feet from the bar and from my friends. Out of the corner of my eye, I saw Kayos snapping in celebration. "YAAASSSSSSSS, Jaimie."

For a split second, I was mortified. Then I realized my friends were truly happy for me. And I hadn't had that kind of attention in a very long time.

After a while, Tiffany and the pretty girl came over to say hi. The girl was Mathias's girlfriend. Clearly, they had an open relationship. Not how I'd ever rolled, but it seemed to work for them.

Mathias gestured to me and told his girlfriend, "If you guess her age wrong, we owe her a drink."

Having a young face my entire life, I had a feeling I would like the results of this game.

Mathias's girlfriend looked at me. "Can I feel your tits?"

Stunned, I agreed.

She put her hands on my chest wall. The color drained from her face. "Are you a *man*?"

"Nope." I said nothing else, wanting to let her squirm for a bit.

She then guessed my age very young.

I got quite a laugh and a Tito's and soda out of the deal. Worked for me.

Mathias asked for my number, and I gave it to him.

We texted the next day, exchanging pleasantries. He lived in a neighboring state, and I didn't expect to see him again.

The following evening, Finn and I drove down to the main student union on campus. It was the place to be on a summer night. Especially the last night of the season.

He ordered a pitcher of beer, and I asked him an important question. "So, the other night, were you hinting at something?"

His brows furrowed, and he shrugged.

"When I offered to give you a ride downtown, and you wanted to repay me. It can be anything you want. Haha," I reminded him.

He smirked, turned his head away, and looked down. "Yeah, I kinda was."

I knew it. I paused and soaked up the moment. "I'm okay with what you're hinting at."

"Good to know. I'm meeting up with friends, but maybe later we can reconvene back at the ranch?"

The ranch? That was too much. I smiled, but inside I was crying laughing.

We sat in silence for a couple awkward minutes. Time for me to go. "All right! I'm gonna go get some food, fix myself a drink, and watch TV."

"Are you going back to binge *13 Reasons Why*?"

Come again? He'd actually remembered what I'd been watching three days ago? Take me on the terrace table right now. Just kidding. I didn't say that. I did give him credit for paying attention though.

A few hours later, he texted to let me know he was still out. Uh, duh. My couch was feet from both the doors into my house, so I would've seen him come in. Then he wanted to talk about what we might do together. Over text. No, sir. No thank you.

Up to that point, I hadn't typed one incriminating thing. Wasn't going to start now. If he wanted to know, he could come back here and figure it out. He knew the address. I finally decided to go to bed. Since I'd gone that far, I made one last point.

Me: If you want a break from the futon, my door isn't locked.

He got home a half hour later and made his way into my pitch-dark room. With the blackout shades, the place was like a cave.

We kissed, and then his hand moved up my pajama top.

Holy shit.

I froze.

He knew I'd had cancer—but not what kind or that I didn't have breasts. Was he going to freak out? Unsure, I freaked out first. "You know there's nothing there, right?" I blurted out.

With zero hesitation, he yelled back, "I don't fucking care."

In that moment, I felt like a new woman. Courtesy of those four words, all my fears of not being desirable disappeared.

The day he left, we said goodbye with a long hug and quick kiss. I wished him well on the next part of his journey, and he was out the door.

Later, I noticed a $20 bill tucked under my wallet on the coffee table. I messaged a picture of it to my queen friend Anita, who replied, "Oh Christ . . . guess it was good." Yes, I'd absolutely shared that picture with the right person. And it had been good. Very, very good.

After work, I drove to the hospital to deliver a flyer for my drag show benefit. The phone dinged with a notification from the room for rent listing. Finn had left me a review. My heart raced. He wouldn't say anything incriminating, would he?

Jaimie is the most gracious host and an amazing person. She went ABOVE AND BEYOND to make me feel welcomed and comfortable. She even took me out a few times and showed me around town. Such a great experience. The space is clean, quiet, private, and spacious. It is located a short drive downtown and a short walk to the beautiful Arboretum. I would highly recommend staying here. Thank you so much for everything and for making my time in Madison unforgettable!

BENEFIT, TAKE TWO

Every month, I looked forward to brunch day with giddy excitement. For the record, I hated cooking. Well, at least for myself. And as far as cleaning went, I'd always rather be doing something else. But I couldn't stand living in filth, so . . . the lesser of two evils. But the night before brunch, I cranked the music and bopped around the house full of energy. While I swept the floors and cleaned the bathroom, I actually smiled. The power of time with friends. Am I right?

One sunny summer Saturday, a big group of us sat around my dining room table and talked about upcoming drag shows.

Liz asked, "Jaimie, are you going to host another benefit?"

I snapped my head toward Dan, who happened to be sitting across the table from me. When in drag, Dan transformed into Broadway diva Lucy, who'd hosted my first drag show benefit.

"I don't know. Lucy, am I going to have another benefit?"

She pulled out her phone and messaged FIVE's owner. In mere minutes, we had a date on the calendar. And got back to our French toast and mimosas.

Days later, I got to work. I wanted to book all the performers for the show. Naturally, I started with those in my first benefit show. Kayos was honored to be included again—as if I wasn't going to have my sister backup dancer in the show. Vanilla radiated joy and love, both on and off stage. Anya brought her very own "dance the house down" energy. And Dee Dee gave the audience comedy queen realness. Luckily, they were all willing to take another chance on a benefit show with me.

The rest of the cast came together beautifully. Shortly after my first benefit show, Amethyst had told me she'd been out of town and wished she could've been a part of it. That meant the world to me. She slayed every time on stage, and I knew she would in my show. And Anita? When I first saw her perform, I couldn't get over her stunning gorgeousness. Then, I got to see her hilarity on stage. I fell in love with Roachie's fun, creative performances during Karizma's Tuesday night "Category Is" shows. After the gift of getting to know her, I got to be a backup dancer during her FIVE Newcomer pageant talent number. Another gift from "Category Is," I laughed so hard I cried when I watched Susan for the first time. Then she sat down to visit with me after the show. I first met Victoria as a bartender at FIVE. Then she took the "Category Is" stage by storm.

After my last radiation session, I set a follow-up appointment with a nurse named Karol. Yes, Karol with a K. The following weekend, Ricky performed in drag for the first time. Her name? Karol with a K. Karol needed to be in my show benefitting that cancer center. Bianca shined in the community. She'd won pageants, hosted drag brunches and the Glitz show downtown, and performed in other benefits for charities.

While I put together an incredible cast, I didn't even think to create a poster. Susan rescued me and offered to make it. We went round and round with backgrounds. Disco ball? Rainbows? Cityscape? All the ideas were fantastic, but not what I wanted. I hoped that the benefit would be about more than me. And more than drag. I landed on the title "Celebrating Life!" Susan asked me what I pictured when I heard "fun" and "life," and what came to mind was a tree full of bright orange leaves next to a path strewn with more orange leaves.

Totally caught her off guard.

Central Park in the fall had gotten me through six weeks of radiation. It needed to be celebrated too. Her inspired design made me misty.

A couple weeks before the benefit, social media notified me of a connection request. Magali Shaw. The name didn't ring a bell. But she was what I liked to call a "FIVE friend request." Someone who has at least twenty-five mutual friends who frequented the nightclub. Magali and I had plenty of friends in common. We'd never met, but sure, we could be friends.

She messaged me to say that as a cancer survivor herself, she was excited for the benefit. At one point, she referred to herself as Mama Shaw. Ummm, lady, that's a little weird. I knew she was old enough to be a lot of these guys' mom. But it didn't occur to me that she truly was "Mama Shaw" and that her son was Demetrius—one of my favorite bartenders. Luckily, I figured that out without too much embarrassment. Until now.

Three weeks before the benefit, I sat through my last Herceptin treatment. When my nurse handed me a bouquet of flowers, my eyes misted over. I'd lived with a port for almost fifteen months, and I hardly noticed it anymore. I didn't feel it under my skin. Some days I forgot I even had it. But I didn't complain when my surgeon suggested removing it three days later. It was time to say goodbye. Presented as a very simple appointment, I did fine until halfway through the procedure.

I realized how lucky I was to be alive and to be having the port removed, then thought about my brother Cory. He didn't get to have this experience. I'm sure his port was removed at some point before he died, but I wasn't going to call his wife to ask for details seven years later. Whenever it had been taken out, it wasn't a celebration of his good health.

Tears streamed down my cheeks. Worried I was making Nathan—the surgeon I hadn't seen in a year—and his resident nervous, I wiped my eyes and stopped crying. As far as I knew, they were doing the procedure flawlessly. I changed the mood in the room with an invitation. "This weekend, I'm hosting a drag show benefit for the cancer center."

"Really? Where?" Nathan wanted details.

"At FIVE Nightclub on the 14th," I shared.

"I'll check my schedule and come if I can," he offered.

The resident showed more excitement. "That's awesome. I'll tell all the other residents about it."

Mission accomplished. I left the room with a smile covering my face and a spring boosting my step.

I'd been personally promoting the benefit for weeks. In the week leading up to the event, my friends stepped up their game. Eddie, one of the greatest drag supporters I've ever met, helped fill the house with her post.

Eddie: I'll be there, YOU SHOULD BE TOO!!! Jaimie has become one great friend of mine, and I'm excited to support such an amazing organization that helped her through a very scary time!! Love is love <heart emoji> Let's celebrate life, eh?! Like, share, and attend this event! #Yuh

For one of the queens in the show's lineup, the cause stretched far beyond me. My heart ached as I read her life's mission.

Bianca: Over 10 years ago I lost my mother to lung cancer. I told myself I would do everything I could to help those in need and search for the cure for cancer. We lose family, friends, and loved ones daily to this deadly disease, and sometimes those lucky ones can pull through and beat cancer. One of those lucky people is my DEAR friend Jaimie Sherling. This one right here is doing amazing work and has put together a fundraiser show for the UW Carbone Cancer Center. I am so excited to be in this 2-part show this coming Saturday at my home club FIVE Nightclub.

On benefit day, I drove to FIVE in the late afternoon. I decorated tables, posted the show lineup in the dressing room, and visited with the queens while they painted themselves. The family-friendly show started at 7 pm.

My teen happily scored a table for two with a theater friend of hers. As much as she argued to change my mind, I wouldn't let her stay for the 18+ show at 9 pm.

My biggest wish was for it to be a packed house and a busy night. It was both. And I finally met Magali in person. So many friends I'd made in the last two years also showed up as well as others who'd come to my first benefit. A friend from South Dakota drove five hours to be there. My favorite chemo nurse came, which wasn't a surprise. We'd connected on social media after she'd taken a new job during my treatment, and she'd RSVP'd.

I buzzed around all night long with hellos, hugs, kisses, all of it. At one point, I rushed to the bar and almost ran into my chemotherapy oncologist. "Dr. Millikan, you're here." If I hadn't had one of the queens paint me that night, I would've started sobbing on the spot.

"The whole crew came!" he said.

Then I saw them—another nurse and two of the people who'd checked me in at the clinic every week for treatment.

The energy that night was electric. Strength, love, and joy shot off the stage during every number. I enjoyed every single performance. My cheeks hurt from smiling all night.

Then Kayos slinked toward the microphone stand in the center of the stage, her silver, satin, floor-length gown and matching headpiece drawing gasps from the audience.

After the first few notes played through the speakers, Lucy spoke into her microphone from a table off stage. "Kayos is dedicating this song to Jaimie and her new life. Yes, she is."

Kayos pointed at me and gave the most incredible performance of the song "Feeling Good."

My eyes welled up, and I fought back the tears. I'd been obsessed with Kayos' talent and beauty from the first time I'd seen her on stage. We locked eyes more than once during the song. I'd never hear it again and not think of her. Thank you again for that number, Kayos.

The rest of the night was a bit of a blur. There were more hugs, lots of pictures, and so much dancing as we all celebrated the hell out of life.

BACK TO BACK

The following weekend, my teenage daughter and I celebrated life again in New York City. Sure, we'd been there a year and a half ago. But that felt like a lifetime ago. I wanted a special trip with her to the city we both loved. And who knows? There could come a time in the not-so-distant future where she wouldn't care about a trip with her mom. I had to take advantage of her interest while it lasted.

The flight there was uneventful—in the best way. By the time we finished the train ride from Newark into the city, we needed pizza. Stat. We couldn't show up to Jen and Kobi's place hangry. After we ate, my daughter met Glory for the first time. I beamed as I watched them play together, mutually fascinated with each other.

That night, my daughter and I went to see *Waitress*. Yes, this was my fourth time. While I cried, it wasn't like with Heather where I couldn't see the stage. With my daughter, I was simply enjoying and sharing a show I adored. We rode the subway uptown in exhausted silence, tiptoed into Jen and Kobi's living room and crashed.

The next morning, I rolled over to the most glorious beams of sunlight filling the room. I didn't even know what time it was. I glanced at my phone and noticed a text from Jen.

Jen: Hey, Jaimie. I went to get coffee and maybe a bite nearby – text me if you need anything otherwise hope you're sleeping well. <heart emoji>

Me: Hey Jen! I was. <heart emoji> Are you still out?

Jen: We got tamales! Coming back.

While the teenager slept in, Jen and I sat on the steps outside her place, where she handed me a warm tamale wrapped in foil. As the scent wafted to my nose, I drooled. Then I ate the most authentic tamale of my life.

Jen also treated me to some cookies, while I gave her life updates I didn't feel comfortable sharing while my daughter was around. I talked about my husband and why we were still married even though our relationship was over in every sense of the word. We'd come to a mutual separation agreement. We weren't even living in the same space anymore. But his job didn't offer health insurance, so I kept him on my coverage.

Jen dropped some wisdom on me, as she often did. "I know you're thinking you're helping him, but could it be that you're hurting him by not giving him the chance to figure this out? And do you really want the nonprofit to be paying for his health insurance?"

Ooof. "Not really, when you put it that way." That conversation changed the course of my life once again. Jen was right about me being in NYC when my life was at a major crossroads.

After Glory woke up from her afternoon nap, we all ventured outside together. We made a necessary stop at Levain Bakery. We walked through Central Park, where I thought of that tree in the ceiling tile I'd looked at for weeks. I laid down in the grass, needing a moment to show gratitude for radiation. My daughter and Glory had their own little picnic together. Cuteness overload.

On our last night in the city, I introduced my daughter to her first piano bar. I felt my brother Cory nudging me to take her to Don't Tell Mama. Personally, I'd say our receipt was on point.

- ✓ Shirley Temple (2)
- ✓ Sexy Mama
- ✓ Ruby Red Slipper

My daughter and I slept the entire plane ride back to Madison. My exhaustion matched my gratitude. I had one work week ahead of me, then even more to celebrate.

The following weekend, KG came to town. After my worst birthday ever, she promised to make my birthday right again. Needless to say, she delivered. It worked out that she arrived the weekend before my actual birthday. What a gift. We had an hour and a half in the car from the Milwaukee airport to Madison to catch up. We had time with the kids. She was their "Auntie KG," after all. She co-hosted brunch and took so many photos. I didn't have one picture of the last three brunches combined. We went to FIVE, and she got to meet the friends she'd been hearing about for years.

PRO TIP: *If you really want to celebrate life, get yourself friends like mine.*

MY DAY: TAKE TWO

As the following week unfolded, I sometimes wondered if I'd made the right decision to not be with my husband anymore. And then I'd be scrolling online and see someone's wisdom. *The right person will come along, and you won't need to do anything to keep them interested, for the simple fact that you'll be enough.*

Okay, why wasn't I tagged in that post?

In the last year, I'd met people who understood how important my birthday was to me. Have you ever been introduced to someone through a group and later can't even pinpoint when or where that was? That sums up Adam, my twenty-something pediatrician friend.

We both knew we'd connected at some point during the summer volleyball season at FIVE. We were immediately friendly and always happy to see each other. Before long, we sat together at shows, and he became the friend I started looking forward to seeing the most. One night, my birthday came up in conversation. I told him he should take me out for an early birthday dinner. Sure enough, he did! The first of many wonderful "date" nights for us.

The night after that first "date," I was back at FIVE for another show. Midnight came, and I mentioned to Jasper, who was standing next to me at the bar, "It's my birthday."

"Ahhhhh. It's your birthday? Want a shot?"

"Sure." Why not start the celebrating ASAP?

The day that followed was a roller coaster. I woke up to countless messages and posts on social media. It was almost overwhelming to feel so loved. Then I ran down to the basement to pop in some laundry. At the bottom of the stairs, my foot squished into soaked carpet. Dammit. An inch of water bubbled up and around the drain. Flooding hadn't been part of my fun birthday plans. But that was life, right? I texted my friend Carla. She had a shop vac at my house within minutes. I carried the tank upstairs and dumped the water outside multiple times. I returned the shop vac and took a steaming hot shower. After that, I treated myself to a retail-therapy spree.

PRO TIP: *Hold onto all the freebie coupons you receive around your birthday to have one huge shopping day.*

That evening, I got to see several friends in a local production of *Mary Poppins*. Stellar way to spend a birthday. The show was over early enough that I wasn't quite ready to end my day. FIVE was literally on the way home. I could stop in. If any of my friends were there, great. If not, I was minutes from home.

I didn't realize it was a special night with a cover charge. Spoiled, most nights I attended shows without paying, and I didn't want to pay if I was leaving.

The door person let me stand there for a minute to decide.

"Jaimie! Happy birthday!" Rob saw me and yelled from behind the bar. "Want a shot?"

"Yes, please!"

Before long, a few friends walked in the back door, and the door person finally said, "Just go in."

Happy birthday to me.

BABY CHICK NO MORE

Cancer had forever changed my body. I'd accepted that. The changes to my hair probably wouldn't last forever, but that journey was more emotional. I thought about my queen friends and their amazing wigs, who followed my hair saga like a season of *RuPaul's Drag Race*. Some remembered my pre-diagnosis natural hair, long and flowing halfway down my back. Many only saw the steady rotation of baby chick/SJP wig/ cute hat.

A couple months after my last chemotherapy treatment, my hair started growing back. I had absolutely no idea how to style short hair. Never mind curly short hair. With encouragement from my queens, I started playing with different styles. The first look was a faux hawk. The sides were still short, but the top tipped over. When Kyle teased me at FIVE that once it started getting longer, he would come up to me and shave the sides again, I figured I was on the right track.

Sure enough, the hair on the very top of my head grew quickly. One night I tried a side swoop. I ran into Karma, who said, "Ah. I am LIVING for this." Yeah, that look stuck for quite some time. Finally, I had enough hair to pull back into the tiniest of ponytails. It reminded me of my daughter as a toddler. Didn't care. I used a hair tie for the first time in over a year. And what did I hear that night at FIVE? "Yaaasssss. Get it, Ponytail." Thank you, Marcos. Your enthusiasm meant the world to me.

Eventually, I needed a haircut. The misshapen mullet was doing me no favors. It would be my first haircut in fifteen months. I thought about my former stylist. I loved seeing her, and she was worth every penny. But I couldn't justify all those pennies considering the competing medical bills. I looked up cosmetology schools in the area, found one about ten minutes away, and called to make an appointment.

A couple days before I was supposed to go, I had a total diva moment. It wasn't fair. I had two college degrees and a full-time job. I should be able to afford a haircut. Yeah, yikes. I decided to get over myself.

As if I wasn't emotional enough on the way, I drove past the clinic where I had that first inconclusive mammogram the spring before. I parked and walked into the salon, determined to make the best of it.

AR introduced himself and led me to the salon chair. "What are you thinking today?"

"I want you to clean it up. It's a bit of a mess."

"Okay, I can do that for you," he assured me.

"Heads up, there might be tears. I had cancer, lost all my hair, and this is my first haircut in a long time." I wanted him to know what he was getting into with me.

He was kind and understanding.

From there, we jabbered about life. "I'm thinking about creating clothing for survivors like me," I shared.

"That's amazing. Do it! You need to go after your dreams. My little brother plays football, and he has a college scout coming to the game this Friday night." He beamed.

Excuse me while I look up that kid to see if he ever played in college. He could be in the NFL by now.

I stood up and admired AR's work in the mirror, grinning sheepishly. "Umm, do you mind if we take a picture together? My friends like to follow my journey," I explained.

"Of course," he said.

I shared so much of my journey, the influencer in me couldn't stop now. Sure enough, my online followers were very interested in this milestone haircut. And my new stylist.

As everyone could've predicted, Jasper kept it the most real. "Tell him to add me."

ONLY TREATS

The weekend before Halloween, I wore my first of three costumes and went out with friends. Yes, you heard right. I had three different costumes that year. Halloween was my favorite holiday. Okay, favorite tied with my birthday. And Halloween with the drag community was like a national holiday. Their commitment was astounding. Derrick was so committed to his Tinman look that he spent hours covering himself in silver body paint.

The best of my three costumes was my reprise of Eleven from *Stranger Things*. In Season 1, Eleven was intriguing and fierce. With her buzzed head, she made the perfect muse for me as a baby chick. In Season 3, Eleven was 100% complete badass. A badass with a bit more hair. Weeks before Halloween, I realized my hair didn't look too different from hers in that season. Then I saw my friend Eddie out one night wearing something that looked like it came out of Eleven's closet. I screamed and begged her to borrow it for Halloween. To no one's surprise, she said yes. I asked her to bring it to brunch, and she did days later. Thanks again, Eddie.

Halloween gave me the complete and total freedom to try on something new. I didn't need anyone's permission, but for some reason I felt like I did. And my time at FIVE, where acceptance of all was the baseline, gave it to me.

Maybe it was Eleven's badassery. Or a newfound feeling of strength and independence. But Jen's wisdom finally sunk in. I wanted a divorce. No, I needed a divorce. Being married, even if only on paper, was a lie. I texted my husband.

Me: Hello. Is there any chance you can give me a call?

A minute later my phone rang.

"Thanks for calling. I didn't want to send this over text." I had zero time to waste. "We both know our marriage has been over for a long time. I would like to file for divorce."

"Okay," he replied.

I hadn't expected an argument . . . but damnnnn. At least I felt validated in my decision.

He did hesitate about something. "Yeah, the only thing was me being on your health insurance."

"I know," I said. "But I don't think keeping you on my insurance at the expense of my mental health is a good idea." In my head, I heard a chorus of YAAASSSSSSS cheering me on.

So, on Halloween, I went to GetDivorcePapers.Com and started the process online. How fitting. It was time for my most favorite costume—a strong, independent woman who needed no man.

KNOW YOUR
WORTH

INCREDIBLE

While I didn't need a man, I wasn't opposed to romantic company. I installed a dating app and made a connection with Mark, who was originally from Australia. He was cute. And funny. Full disclosure, I was intrigued by the accent. Early on, he made it clear that he was only looking for an fwb-type of situation.

I'd never explored the friends with benefits scenario. Not judging anyone else who made that choice, but it had never been a plan of mine. My first brother got married when I was fourteen. I became an aunt the following year. Before I graduated high school, three of my brothers and sisters were married. I looked at their wedding photos proudly displayed in the living room every day. In my mind, you dated to find a future spouse and parent for your children. It's what you did. Those plans worked out. Sort of. Why not try something different? It only needed to be safe and consensual.

After a bit of messaging on the app, Mark got right to the point.

Mark: Would you like to meet first or just dive right in?

Me: Let's meet first. I'm not *that* easy.

A couple days later, we met for tea. We hit it off, made pleasant conversation, and he was a complete gentleman. To be sure that wasn't a fluke, we met for tea one more time. We talked and laughed for an hour. Worked for me. I invited him over to my house during lunch hour—perk of working from home—and mentioned it to a close coworker. She was happy for me. "Ooooo," she said. "You're going to have a funch. A fun lunch. Good for you."

A few days later, I had dinner with one of my favorite couples—Max and Boone. We always had fun together at FIVE. I needed to spend more time in their company. We talked about my business—both the clothing line business and my dating business. That included my new friend from Australia.

"Tell me everything." Typical Max.

So, I spilled about my funch.

"Oh my God. You had a nooner?"

Yeah, Max, that needed to be screamed across the restaurant.

But with his exuberant question, there was no judgment. He was a constant cheerleader in my life. Always wanted the best for me. Always came from a place of love. Almost always in caps lock.

The day after my second funch, I got a message from Mr. Australia.

Mark: Hey there. Happy Wednesday. Listen, I've been thinking about our fwb situation and wanted to let you know that I'll be calling it off. <insert rambling cliché after cliché>

Nothing that meant anything to me.

Mark: Something just seems off, that sounds weird I know but I'm going to go with my gut on this. This is definitely my issue and not yours. You've been great and I have enjoyed our time but, that, I think, has come to an end. I'll keep it brief and wish you well. All the best.

Yes, those thirteen lines of text kept it very brief. Well done, good sir. But for some stupid reason, it messed with my head. I wished it hadn't. I allowed myself to go down the "what's wrong with me?" rabbit hole. I'd agreed to fwb. I'd kept it casual. I'd rocked a hilarious gif game. If the sex was terrible, why had he come back a second time?

I leaned on my amazing friends, who were willing to talk through the crazy with me. They were probably right that I'd been starting to develop feelings for Mark and maybe that freaked him out. Or maybe he couldn't handle the lack of breasts but wasn't able to say that out loud. The age old "it's not me, it's him" won out. Cut print. Moving on.

The last time I'd dated, three billion years ago, ghosting was a foreign concept. I mean, even if you got dumped, there was still a good chance you'd see the guy in the high school hallways every day. Fast forward to this century. Ghosting drove me crazy. I chatted with someone for hours, thought we had a connection, and their account was deleted the next day. Good times.

But I tried to stay hopeful. My next date after Mark, though? It was like a job interview. Question. Answer. Question. Answer. The only time I laughed was when *I* said something funny.

That night, I was complaining to Max about my date and showed him a picture for reference.

"He looks like a serial killer," Max said. "Goodbye." He knew I deserved better. He knew I was spending time and energy engaging in meaningful conversation, only to be ghosted. It was emotionally exhausting. He didn't think dating apps were the right move for me now. He looked me in the eye and said something I will never forget. "If he doesn't kiss you like this, he's not worth it."

Bam. He kissed me right then and there.

Holy. Hell. I mean, wow. Amazing kiss. Boone was a lucky guy.

The next day, I playfully reminded Max of our passionate moment.

Me: I kind of hate that being my best kiss in YEARS.

Max: WE KISSED????? That's incredible.

I agreed.

ONE IN A MILLION?

I'd never been much of an impulse buyer. At all. Especially clothing. I can't remember how many times I wore my brothers' and sisters' hand-me-downs growing up. It was a way of life being the sixth child. Being frugal stuck.

But one day, I stumbled onto the most amazing shirt online. "In a World of Tens, Be an ELEVEN." The font mimicked the *Stranger Things* logo, obviously. I had to have it. I ordered it and impatiently waited for weeks. When it finally arrived, I paired it with a silver sequin pencil skirt. Because why not wear a T-shirt and a silver sequin skirt on a random Thursday night?

I arrived at FIVE and walked toward the darts area. There was always a fun crowd over there.

Kayos stopped in her tracks when she saw me. "If that isn't the most 'know your worth' shirt?"

Right? I wholeheartedly agreed. Then I thought about the number of times she'd used that hashtag in the last year. It finally clicked. I appreciated the inspiration to quite literally own my value.

Thanks to that shirt, as an Eleven, I felt more confident about my dating prospects. By that weekend, I had a dinner on the calendar. He canceled the morning of. I respected the upfront communication. It was a little absurd to give props for that common courtesy, but I'd found that common courtesy and online dating often didn't coexist.

That afternoon, a guy named Mike reached out. We'd been messaging for a couple days but hadn't made plans to get together yet.

Mike: What are you up to tonight?

Me: Not much, going to a drag show later. How about you?

Mike: Just finished at the studio. Some of the brogas and I are going for a drink.

Yes, he typed brogas. As in, dudes who did yoga together.

Mike: You should come out and meet us.

I wasn't sure if he was joking or not. But who cared? Public place, no time like the present, and I was free. I dolled myself up a bit and drove to the bar. It was a fun first meeting, and we went on a few dates.

One night out, I paired my cute dress with my favorite fragrance mist.

"That smells good." He leaned toward me.

"Thanks. It's called *One in a Million* 'cause that's what I am." I slyly smiled, feeling extra sassy and confident. And maybe a little tipsy.

He shot back, "Yeah, but it's actually not one in a million at all. They're mass produced. That many of exactly the same product came off the assembly line."

Wow, way to kill the mood, dude. I should've known then we wouldn't go much further. Whatever we didn't have going on fizzled out after one more date.

A couple weeks later, I was wearing the same scent out at FIVE. My friend Kavon told me how good I smelled. I rattled off the story about Mike. Kavon stopped me mid-sentence, put up his hand in argument, and corrected me. "Uhh, one in a *billion*."

What was that the queens always said about knowing you worth?

A CARAMEL HOLIDAY

A few weeks before Thanksgiving, I caught up with Ben after a show at FIVE.

"Do you have plans for the holiday?" he asked.

Of all the holidays, I dreaded being alone on Thanksgiving. For me, that day was all about gathering with people you loved and sharing good food. While I wasn't afraid to eat alone, I wasn't about to cook Thanksgiving dinner for myself. "Ummm." Caught off guard, I stammered. "I don't know. I might be spending it with my friend Heather."

"Okay. Well, if you don't go with her, you're welcome to join my family."

I made a note in my phone to check in with Heather. Last Thanksgiving, I'd had a great time celebrating with her family. But we hadn't talked about this year yet.

I called her that afternoon. "I keep forgetting to ask what you're doing for Thanksgiving this year. I wasn't sure if I could crash again."

"I'm so glad you asked. I'm going to celebrate with my boyfriend's family. If not, you totally could've joined us again."

I told her I understood, and messaged Ben.

Me: Heyyyy! Heather is going to be out of town for Thanksgiving. I would absolutely love to join your family. Thank you for asking!! <heart emoji>

Ben: Perfect! I will let my mom know and send you more information.

Me: <my favorite per-fect gif> Thank you, and tell your mom thank you from me too!

Ben: Of course!

Thrilled to be included and wanting to make the very best impression on Ben's family, I baked them my famous caramel bars. When I arrived, I was warmly greeted by his parents, his brother, his sister, and her husband. I instantly felt like part of the family. Ben's invitation was such a gift. Never mind being spoiled.

His mom took my coat, and I joined everyone around the kitchen island.

His dad asked the important question. "Jaimie, would you like a caramel apple martini?"

"Absolutely." Who would say no to that? That drink was decadent.

As I nibbled on appetizers, Ben handed me a strip of paper and a pen. "Write down five things you're thankful for."

Okay. That didn't take long.

We sat down to eat, and the papers were folded and put into a basket. Every person took a paper, read the list, and the rest of the table guessed who wrote it.

I smiled and held back tears. I was so honored to be included in their special day and that tradition. And the food was amazing.

We took a short food break and dove into dessert. Afterward, we shuffled down to the basement and played *What Do You Meme?* together.

I was invited to drink more, which I politely declined. "I still need to drive myself home."

Ben's mom offered, "You can sleep here. We have room."

Thanks, Mom, but I was going to sleep in my own bed.

She insisted on sending me home with a full container of the entire meal.

I did my best to spread the love by leaving my caramel bars for them.

The next day Ben's boyfriend, Craig, texted me.

Craig: Btw

Craig: I'm mad at you.

Oh no. What did I do? Had I said something offensive after that second carameltini? Luckily, the next text popped up to answer my questions.

Craig: Do you know how many of these goddamn bars I've eaten?

That sounded about right. There was a reason I only made a pan if I planned on sharing with a group. A large, hungry group.

I sat back and smiled. Even without the caramel drizzle, it had been my favorite Thanksgiving holiday in a very long time. Thanks again, Ben.

NEW CHAPTER

I finished my Thanksgiving leftovers and turned the page to December. As my friends' family Christmas pictures popped up on social media, I prepared to go to the courthouse and officially file for divorce.

As I got dressed to go to FIVE, I remembered the shirt I'd found at Upshift Swap Shop months earlier—a simple black tee, with "Guac Over Guys" written in large block lime-green letters. With my abysmal dating life, I felt like the shirt was made specifically for me. And my friends loved it as I stood at the bar.

Max noticed first. "Oh, that"—he pointed to my shirt—"is a full mood."

Smiling, I turned to Boone. "Can I ask a favor?"

"Of course," he answered. "What can I do for you?"

I wasn't questioning my decision to get divorced. But the roller coaster had so many ups and downs, I needed to take care of myself. Specifically, I needed a plan for the day I filed, and he worked at a hotel blocks from the courthouse. "Next Wednesday, I file for divorce."

"Oh gosh, I'm so sorry."

"It's okay," I said. "But thank you. Can I valet my car at the hotel that morning?"

He offered a resounding, "Yes."

On a freezing December morning, I met my husband at the courthouse. We stood at the window next to each other, and I handed over the paperwork I'd prepared. We walked outside together and stood awkwardly on the sidewalk.

He hugged me. "I'm sorry about everything."

"Me too." I didn't have the energy to say anything more.

Afterward, I walked around the capitol square and treated myself to breakfast. I didn't take the day off from work. That left way too many hours to obsess about why our marriage failed. But I also didn't want to race back home. Work laptop bag slung over my shoulder, I headed over to a coffee shop. I put in my earbuds, listened to great music, and had a productive morning there.

To end my time downtown, I had to go back and get my car at the hotel. A great excuse to give them some business, I sat myself down at the hotel bar. Boone had recently posted a picture of a pear martini. I ordered that and some fries. The glass set in front of me was as striking as it was in the photo. I toasted myself. To a new chapter and to my valiant efforts in self-care.

I decided on a fashionable new life chapter. Time to kick my clothing business into high gear. Nancy helped me submit my prototype pattern to a manufacturer. While I waited for an estimate, I knew I needed to spread the word about my line.

The following morning, I woke up earlier than I had in months. In my best skirted suit, I drove to a local chamber of commerce event. I still wasn't ready to announce my business on social media, but I could network and tell people to watch for it. The perk of the early start? The meeting would be over before my day job started.

My page-a-day calendar confirmed my effort. *You will have to say no to things to say yes to your work. It will be worth it.* Sure, Lin-Manuel Miranda. And your work has been validated by whom exactly? Wait. By KG. She'd bought the calendar for me. Also, the Tony Awards Administration Committee.

That being said, it wasn't going to be all work and no play. Adam asked if I would be a backup dancer for Electra. Hell yes, I would. Honored to be asked. That Friday night, I went over to Adam's to learn the choreography. It was such a blast. One of the best Friday nights I've had in a very long time. Good thing it was fun, since I could barely move my arms the next morning.

I practiced the choreography every day leading up to the show. If I was going to be in black fishnets and a bodysuit on stage in front of my friends, I needed to nail the dance moves.

The night of the show, I sauntered on stage and popped my hip. When my friends in the audience realized it was me, the screams erupted. I even got a dollar bill from Bryanna. Life goal achieved.

Only a few pages in, this new chapter sounded pretty great to me.

BOYS, GIRLS, OR EVERYBODY?

On a freezing Friday night, I raced into FIVE excited to start my weekend, see my friends, and watch a drag show. Just inside the door, I saw Derrick. He brought his cousin and their friend Quinn. I'd met both of them at Derrick's fundraiser the month before. I hugged everybody and told them, "Nice to see you again."

Later in the evening, I wanted to dance. I happened to be near Quinn. "OMG, I love this song. Let's dance!" And off we went.

After a little bit, she asked, "You want a shot?"

"Why not?" A friend of Derrick's was a friend of mine, right?

Two days later, I was back at FIVE to finish off my Sunday Funday. Derrick and company were there again. I decided to go for it—when Derrick was alone. "Does Quinn like girls, boys, or everybody?" I asked him.

"Well . . . she's actually experimenting right now."

"Okay. Well, I'm asking for a reason."

"Then you should come sit at the bar with us."

I walked over with Derrick and joined the group.

After a little while, Quinn asked a loaded question. "Jaimie, do you come up to Appleton not for fundraisers?"

"I could."

Derrick almost spit out his entire drink.

Minutes later, I headed to the bathroom. On my way out, I saw Quinn walking in my direction. I specifically do not say toward me because she was in a main crossroads in the bar and could've been going to the bathroom, outside, or to the dance floor. So, I asked her. "Hey, where are you going?"

"I was going to the bathroom to make out with you."

About face. I walked back into the bathroom, and she followed. We squeezed into the first stall, and I locked it behind us. Since nothing physical had ever happened with Victoria, it was my first time really kissing a female.

And I liked it. And yes, I heard that Katy Perry song in my head too.

OUT TONIGHT

As Christmas approached, I struggled emotionally. My immediate family lived across the country, and my children spent that holiday with their dad and his family. In my day-to-day life, I didn't mind being single. But for some reason, being alone during the holidays presented a challenge for me.

And along came Brandon's Friendsmas invite.

Please join us on Christmas Day around 3:00 pm if you would like! We know many do not go home for Christmas or you are back early so come join us at Karol's (Ricky's) beautiful apartment with plenty of space for all!

I couldn't click on "accept" fast enough.

Me: Thank you for inviting me for Christmas! <crying emojis> < heart eyes emojis>

Brandon: Oh stahp! Of course!

Me: It means a lot to me, and I'll cry if I want to!

Brandon: Why are you so honored to be invited? Lol. You're like family to so many of us.

Whaaaaaa.

The Saturday before Christmas, Liz and Jess joined me for the *Snow Queen Drag Brunch* at Pasture & Plenty. They'd maybe met one time before, and we looked like the three musketeers that day. The power of drag to bring people together. Also, delicious food and craft cocktails didn't hurt.

PRO TIP: *If you were friends with the queens and Santa was one of your best friends, you may end up with a fantastic picture on Santa's lap.*

On Christmas Eve Eve, I cleaned up from dinner and sat down on the couch. Ready to relax for the evening, I was surprised to hear from Beth. She taught me in drum corps as a teenager. Our lives ran in opposite directions most of the time, but we could always pick up and talk like no time had passed.

Beth: Are you around tomorrow evening?

Me: I was thinking of going to FIVE. Why do you ask?

Beth: We might like to drop something off for you! Just go with it . . . when are you going to FIVE?

Me: Let's say around 9.

Beth: We'll be there before then!

Finally, I turned the calendar page to Christmas Eve. I wouldn't have my children—I was used to that—but it was my first Christmas Eve without a romantic partner since I'd turned eighteen. Not that it was terrible to be alone. It just felt strange.

Pushing past the weirdness, I pretended like it was another weekday and decided to use the "free time" to my advantage. I drove to a coffee shop, treated myself to a chai tea latte, and worked on my business plan. Thanks, Entrepreneurial Training Program. That evening, I posted about the entire day.

It's my first Christmas Eve completely alone in a very long time. Kinda weird. But really, I wasn't alone at all. I chatted/texted with some fabulous friends. I went to the store and was handed a bouquet of flowers. Beth, Dan, and their kids randomly stopped by to gift me a Danish puff. This afternoon, I headed to my favorite coffee shop (thanks to two more amazing friends for that gift card!) I got to WORK on my business plan. 2020, I'm coming for you!

Within minutes, I got a message.

Karizma: Come to FIVE.

I hadn't posted for pity. Or an invite. I mean, I was already planning on going. I was simply processing my day, which I'd been doing more and more over the last couple years. But it felt great to be asked. I went and had an amazing time.

I visited with Lucy as "Out Tonight" from *Rent* blasted through the speakers. "I LOVE this song!!" I belted the lyrics, then told her, "Kayos said I needed to perform this sometime."

"Do you want to be in my show?" she asked.

"Yes!" I screamed. Yes. Yes. Yes. And with that one random conversation, I was booked in my first drag show. On stage, by myself, and not as a backup dancer.

I might've been single on Christmas Eve, but I was definitely not alone.

ROAR

Earlier in December, Max had invited me to a dinner party to celebrate the one-year anniversary of Boone moving to Wisconsin. I'd had my kids. Only having them half-time, I didn't like to make plans when they were with me. But Max had told me to bring them, and I had. My friends were lovely people.

The food had been amazing, and the kids went along with being the only teens there. Somehow, the conversation had steered to New Year's Eve. My friends told me I *had* to be at FIVE for the Roaring '20s party. Of course, I'd wanted to go, but the kids had been scheduled to be with me then too. So began a rousing debate between my friends and my daughter over leaving a group of teenagers home alone that night for a respectable amount of time while I stopped at FIVE to toast the new year. My heart had grown ten sizes bigger watching my friends and my daughter work together toward a common goal.

Before New Year's Eve, I connected with the parents of the kids coming to my house and got the okay to duck out for an hour. I put on my black flapper dress and headband and drove over to FIVE.

The place was packed, and it was a rush to see so many friends in one place. We counted down with the promise that 2020 was going to be amazing, and I knew I was exactly where I was supposed to be. I then raced around saying my goodbyes and left to pick up my other teen at a friend's house.

If that wasn't a standard roaring night, I don't know what was.

DO BETTER

After a particularly long and stressful work week, a group of friends and I headed to a nearby piano bar. I'd had so much fun at the one in New York with my daughter, I was long overdue to visit another in my backyard.

The night flew by. I was having a great time. Might've had a couple drinks. Which led to an urgent need to go to the bathroom.

The women's restroom was fully occupied.

I crossed my legs, but that wasn't going to cut it. My bladder was as full as my martini glasses had been before I drank them. In desperation, I decided to use the men's room. I'd done it before, and everyone had survived. I figured I would look at nothing, beeline to a stall, take care of business, and beeline my way out.

As I walked in, two men applauded me.

"You ROCK!" they yelled.

On my way out, though, I realized I'd made one man very angry.

"This is a *men's* room," he said. "You can't be in here!"

Trying to calm him down, my "it's just a bathroom" did the exact opposite.

"No, it's not! It's a *men's* room!"

I went on my way, not wanting to create a scene or upset him more.

Later that evening, I really had to go again. And the line for the women's restroom snaked out the door and down the hall. My bladder wouldn't be able to hold it that long.

Did I have a right to use the men's room?

No.

But was it really the end of the world if I did?

Apparently, yes.

I walked out of the bathroom and an employee stopped me. "You're done. You need to leave the building."

I stared at him confused, unable to speak.

"Someone made a formal complaint," he added.

A formal complaint? Really? Since I'd been there for hours, I decided it was best to leave. But not before I asked, "Is it your official policy that people must use the correct re-stroom?"

On my way out, something in my brain snapped. I thought again about how I didn't have breasts. I didn't have the body parts that made many women identify as female. I proceeded to say this to my angel of a friend who'd left with me. As I cried on her shoulder, I grieved again for what I lost because of cancer.

I wouldn't go back and do implants—and no judgment on anyone who makes that choice—but that didn't mean that I didn't still wish for the breasts I'd had two summers earlier.

Side note: That policy about using the "correct" restroom? Who was that staff person to make a judgment about my gender? What if I'd been transgender? What if I'd been in the middle of transitioning? In 2020, businesses needed to do better.

NEW PATH

I'd matched with Hector on a dating app a few days before I'd have my kids for a week. Conversation started off well, and he suggested going out that weekend. We compromised with a coffee date the following week, and he texted me every single day. He seemed eager to get to know me, which I appreciated.

The chai time was lovely. He complimented my beauty more than once. No complaints there. When I explained why I wasn't married anymore, he reached out to touch my hand. By the time I got back to my office that afternoon, there was a text waiting for me.

Hector: Thank you for a lovely time <red heart emoji>

We went out for dinner the following week, and I cooked him dinner the week after that. We talked about being exclusive and the fact that neither of us were communicating romantically with anyone else. He was preparing to go to California for a few weeks for work. At first, I wasn't too happy with that prospect. But the more I thought about it, I realized I could use that time wisely. Having my kids every other week, it would really only be a couple weeks of not seeing Hector. I had plenty to do for my business and would be busy.

I'd researched multiple manufacturers and waited for quotes. The startup fees staggering, I needed a different plan. I searched for local seamstresses willing to take on a new project. Like I said, plenty to keep me busy.

Early in the day, Hector texted me a picture of the special tea mug contraption he'd told me about the night before.

I returned the favor and shared about what sparked joy in my life.

After that, I got crickets. Not even a lame emoticon for almost a week.

I didn't get it. He'd texted me daily when we first matched. Tired of waiting and wondering, I reached out to him.

Me: Hey, hope the weekend with the kids has been good. Things seem different since Tuesday. Am I imagining that?

Hector: Sorry Jamie I feel like i am in a different stage now. Not sure if i am up for dating. You are wonderful, probably just not the right time for me. Wish you the best.

First of all, how hard was it to spell someone's name right? Or capitalize a few "I's" for crying out loud. And not up for dating? Seriously? Great idea to be on an app then saying you were. Interesting too that you were in a different stage when you sat in my house and talked about being exclusive.

I felt like I was back in high school. Boys always broke up with me and never explained why. At least not anything I understood. Oy.

I was angry. Confused. Frustrated. I'd put mental and emotional energy into the conversations. Yes, conversations which were messages on an app. But that was me. Unsure if I would ever find a romantic partner, I had a complete meltdown. Not so much a "woe is me, and someone please pay me a compliment right this minute" moment. More like a "this is a real possibility for my future" moment. Grieving that loss, I cried a lot that day.

That night, I dumped a bunch of what had happened on Adam.

"You need to get off that app!" Fired up, inches from my face, he yelled at me.

Whoa. Take a breath, my friend. I wasn't quite convinced, but I was listening. I knew that it came from a place of love.

"I just don't think it's right for you."

A while later, I drove him home and parked the car in front of his place.

He looked me in the eyes and held my hands. "You're going to find someone. You're funny. You're amazing. You're *gorgeous*."

My heart skipped a beat. How was it that yet another human who had no sexual attraction to me whatsoever made me feel the most incredible?

During all of that, my phone chimed nonstop.

Max had a lot to say as well. Well, he had a lot to type.

Max: Hi I LOVE you. You're incredible, and you're going to find exactly the right guy for you! The conundrum you're dealt with is – do you go all in for every guy you get a good vibe from and wait for it to stick? OR do you become more selective and wait for a man who's WORTH your 100%? The choice is completely yours, and I will ALWAYS love and support you either way <heart emojis>

Me: Maybe it's the right girl?

Max: BITCH MAYBE. NEVER discount the fact that you grew up in a time where homosexuality was definitely not something to be talked about. And that perhaps an attraction to women has always been there but muffled and suffocated by society's rules. Be it a man or woman, there's somebody out there for you. <heart emojis> Like, statistically even. There are literally BILLIONS of people on this earth, there's gotta be SOMEONE out there for you. The question is how much energy and time are you willing to give the ones who aren't for you? And I will say, it's a learning experience and "builds character" <eyeroll emoji> every time it doesn't work out. Every trial and tribulation comes with a lesson you can learn from to prepare yourself for the future. But you've built enough character. Again, not to be crass, but you lost your BREASTS and a HUSBAND within a year. And you don't need men letting you down or teaching you to be stronger or more emotionally withheld or whatever. You gotta find someone who's on that same wavelength, who's been through some shit themselves (maybe not the same shit, but comparative trials and tribulations) and build from there. And in your LIFE—the divorce and breast cancer were HUGE wake up calls. You're actively trying to better yourself and start a business. These 6'5" Australian hotties can't even relate. Find someone on your path. <heart emoji>

And . . . the dating app was deleted by the time I finished brushing my teeth.

DATE WHO?

With Valentine's Day right around the corner, I was over it. I'd never been a fan of the holiday. I found it over-commercialized. Enough with the hearts, candy, and jewelry ads. If you didn't have a date, what were you even doing with your life?

In a shocking twist, social media spun the holiday and made my month. One of my social media apps prompted me to fill in this blank, *I deserve a date with* _____, where you typed in @ and filled in the blank with the third name that popped up. Adam and I both did it and got each other. Naturally. No wonder we referred to each other as #soulmates. With so much focus on romance, I loved the idea of dating my friends. I let everyone know with this post.

> *So, if anyone wants to go on a date with me, please just ask. If you don't live near me and come to Madison, I'll take you on a date. And not just this month. Love doesn't expire on February 15th. I want this to continue all year long. Let's do this, friends!*

My friend Patrick specifically caught me off guard with his comment: Levi wants a date.

I thought he was clever to use his nickname. Patrick and I had met at a volunteer event and reconnected on social media at the beginning of the year. But I didn't think too much of it. The whole point was dating friends.

A few days later, I opened a box of cookies, took a video, and posted it as a boomerang on social media before heading to FIVE.

By the time I parked my car in the lot, I saw a message notification from Patrick.

Patrick: Omg MY FAVORITES!!!

Me: Ummm of COURSE. You have excellent taste.

Friendly banter. Fun. Totally happy to keep it going.

Patrick: Well yeah . . . I'm talking to YOU after all . . .

Hmm, was this getting extra friendly? Totally okay with that too.

Except the conversation slowed to a grinding halt.

A week later, he messaged me again.

Patrick: "Omg I am too slow replying to messages. Can I be old-fashioned and call you sometime?"

Sure, why not? I'd had fun chatting with him when we'd volunteered way back when.

I also didn't sit around waiting for the phone to ring. First thing that Saturday morning, I primped myself for a photo-shoot date. Finally ready to share my clothing line with the world, I met Susan Elizabeth in the lobby of a swanky hotel downtown.

"Well, hello, gorgeous," she greeted me.

"Hello to you, gorgeous."

"Are you ready for this?"

"Absolutely. What's the plan?"

"Well, I want to get some shots here in the lobby. Maybe head over to the capitol in a bit?"

"I love it."

Susan got to work making me feel like a supermodel. After she exhausted her ideas in the lobby, she wished out loud, "It's too bad we can't go up to the restaurant."

"My friend Kyle works there. Let me see if he's working today." I retrieved my phone and texted him.

Me: Hey! Are you at work now? I'm in the building, wanted to say hi quick.

Kyle: I am. Where are you?

Me: In the elevator coming up <grin emoji>

The elevator dinged, and Kyle greeted me with a quick kiss and hug.

"Kyle, this is Susan. She's taking pictures for my launch."

"You're welcome to take some shots up here. We open at 5."

"Thank you so much," I replied.

"Have fun," he said, and off he went.

Susan took full advantage of the space.

I sat on a couch by the fireplace with a cocktail in my hand. I posed on the balcony with the capitol building behind me. And she made my brand look good.

After hugs and kisses goodbye, I raced to my car. I had another date that evening—Pride Prom. I'd enjoyed my high school prom, but it wasn't a magical night. And now that dress with the poufy sleeves made me cringe.

For this prom, the perfect dress already hung in my closet. I'd bought a form-fitting silver sequin dress back in November for no other reason than it reminded me of Serena van der Woodsen. Bonus points for being on sale. I'd had no idea when I'd wear it. I knew it begged to be worn with friends.

I got dressed, touched up my hair and makeup, and Magali picked me up. We went downtown for a drink, then hopped onto the shuttle to the winery for prom.

Weeks before, my friend Tiffany had asked me to save a dance for her there. Okay, cool. I danced with friends. But after she brought it up a few times, I started to think about her differently. Maybe this prom night would have some romance after all.

While I sat on the bumpy shuttle, my phone pinged.

Tiffany: Are you almost here?!

Butterflies surfaced in my stomach. Wow, she was really excited to see me.

Minutes inside the door, our eyes met. I crossed the room to her. We hugged.

Then, she introduced me to her date.

And . . . I felt like a complete idiot. I avoided her for the rest of the evening. In the final hour of the prom, I let my emotions get the best of me—by sitting down for a few minutes.

Jacob noticed. "Is everything okay?"

"I'm just having a bit of a moment being here and single." I started to tear up.

"That's not what tonight is about," he responded. "You have five minutes. You can cry for five minutes, then you're done with it."

I didn't want to take anything away from his night. "Okay." I took a walk to the bathroom, sat in the stall, set a timer on my phone, and cried for exactly five minutes. I stood up, wiped my eyes, and walked back to the dance floor. I held it together in the building. On the shuttle ride back, I cried on Magali's shoulder.

Once again, I'd struck out at romance but grand-slammed in the friend department.

QUARANTINE BRAIN

Life went on.

Sort of.

Mostly.

Okay, not really.

The next Friday afternoon, I picked up my daughter after school, and a few of her friends hopped into the car. Sleepover fun awaited. I stopped to pick up a few pizzas. As soon as I pulled into the parking lot, Adam called me.

"Heyyyyy," I answered, per usual.

"Did you hear they're closing schools next week?"

How did my single, childless, twenty-nine-year-old friend know about the school district's plans before I did? Well, he was a pediatrician. But still.

Okay, so the kids got an extended spring break. We could lay low for a couple weeks.

Businesses operated as usual. That Sunday night, I drove to FIVE for the MadCity Drag Revue. I pulled on the back-door handle. Locked. It wasn't a benefit show, so it didn't make sense that I couldn't get in that way. The sign on the door explained, per health services guidelines, that everyone needed to be counted and the patrons limited to fifty.

Okay. Maybe not so usual.

But inside, it felt like any other Sunday night—until the show was over, and we were reminded that the bar was closing at midnight, over two hours early. 12:01 am was considered a new day. Everyone could leave, reenter, and be counted to fifty again. Not worth it. FIVE cleared out minutes after midnight.

The next afternoon, FIVE's owner went live on social media and shared he was closing indefinitely. I couldn't control my emotions. Two tiny dams broke behind my eyes. They were my family, and I had no idea when I was going to see them again.

Patrick called me a few days later.

Grateful for a distraction, I kept him company on the phone as he drove to a concert.

By the time he arrived, he'd shared that he was traveling on business for a few days. Basically, letting me know he'd be off the grid.

I didn't need this information, but I also didn't mind the openness.

While he sat in the airport waiting to board the plane, he started messaging again. He made a comment about my Pride Prom dress.

I mean, can you really go wrong with form-fitting silver sequins? He clearly felt more than friendly feelings toward me, and it was mutual.

After he landed, he called on his drive home. Two hours flew by quickly.

Over the next few weeks, we spoke a handful of times. The conversations were easy. We made each other laugh, and we were both attracted to each other physically.

One night, I was complaining about back pain.

"I could fix that for you," he offered.

"If only we weren't in the middle of a global *pandemic*," I shot back.

We got off the phone a few minutes later. I washed my face and turned on the radio. "Fix You" came on. Was that ironic or flat out creepy?

Our communication was very sporadic over the next few weeks. When he messaged me, I responded fairly quickly. I did with everyone. But he might respond that day or three days later. What bothered me about it was that he still had time to post long soliloquies on social media every day about gratitude. A lovely practice, don't get me wrong. Being full of gratitude is good for the soul. But come on, really? You could write a short novel, but you couldn't respond to a message? To quote the incomparable Olivia Pope, "If you want me, earn me!"

A few days later, he set a specific time to call me. I appreciated the advance planning. Well into the evening, I got a text.

Patrick: The crew wants to watch a movie with me tonight . . .

I completely understood making that a priority. But it still didn't feel great. Why had he even planned to talk to me while he was at work? I was beginning to feel like a convenient distraction to him, and I didn't like it.

I messaged Max. He had a way of listening, responding with hysterical one-liners, and giving great advice. But I was not expecting the truth bombs he dropped on me.

Max: If you really think boys are necessary, you have a lot to evaluate about yourself and your own mental health.

We went from messages to a video call. "Jaimie, I love you."

"I love you too, Max."

"Right now, you seem to latch onto anyone who would give you attention." He never minced words.

OUCH.

"Romantic attention feels different than friend attention. I miss the spark," I explained.

"You're not looking for that fun, flirty attention. You're looking for that to be long term, and that's hard to find. Especially now."

"I'm alone all the time. It's too much."

"I know. And it's hard."

"It really is."

"Hang in there. You can do this. Time for bed."

"Good night, Max."

In a matter of minutes, I was fast asleep. First thing in the morning, I turned on the radio. I liked to jam while I washed my face. "Sit Still, Look Pretty" came on. Even though I'd heard those lyrics countless times, I felt like I was hearing them for the first time. Truly "this queen don't need a king." Holy hell. How did it not occur to me until then that Patrick's last name was *King*?

Blame it on quarantine brain.

SAFER AT HOME?

When coronavirus turned the world upside down, my professional life didn't change. I'd worked from home for the last seven years. But this felt different. Pre-pandemic, I'd lived two very different lives outside of the workday. During my weeks with the kids, our evenings were busy with homework, dinner, and extra-curricular activities. When I didn't have the kids, my evenings were busy with fun and friends.

One day it hit me. I'd made it to 5 pm and managed to stay focused at work all day. But from now until bedtime? I could read or go for a walk. And for the record, I often did both. But damn, I missed being with other people. Crazy as it might sound, quarantine was harder for me in some ways than my cancer treatment.

Was I minimizing the experience of having cancer? Absolutely not. I did say *my* cancer journey. During my treatment, I'd never experienced isolation. I'd never been physically alone if I didn't want to be. And now, I had to be alone—for an indefinite amount of time. If I could've planned, if I knew when we'd be "back to normal," it might've been easier. Some days, I coped better than others.

March 29th was a day I'd mark in the better column. Derrick and I had gotten our tickets to see *Wicked* the previous October. I couldn't wait to see it again. Part of me wanted to create a new memory. The last time I saw it, my ex-husband proposed to me before the show.

Derrick and I messaged each other as it got closer. We daydreamed about where we'd go for dinner and cocktails beforehand. How much fun we'd have.

Wicked arrived in early March, and friends posted from the theater. I could not wait. On March 14th, Derrick delivered the news.

Derrick: They canceled the rest of the *Wicked* shows <thirty-six crying face emojis>

Me: <twenty-eight crying face emojis>

Derrick: I'm so sad!

Me: Me too!

Disappointed as I was, I understood. By the time our original show date came, I decided to enjoy it anyway. I slipped on my silver sequin dress, poured myself a cocktail in my *Wicked* cup, and listened to the entire Broadway cast recording. Thanks again, Spotify.

While I missed seeing and hugging my friends, coronavirus reminded me of who my closest friends were. Pre-pandemic, Marcos and I had seen each other often out at FIVE. We went to the same shows and were always friendly to each other. I could count on him for a smile and a hug. Earlier in the winter, I'd sat down next to him at the bar and finally had a conversation that changed everything. We dove into family relationships, acceptance . . . real talk. There was a moment he apologized for it being too heavy. It wasn't. Not for a second. I despised small talk. Really getting to know each other was wonderful. I was so grateful for his friendship and for all the times he checked in on me throughout the quarantine.

PRO TIP: *Keep a friend close who greets you daily with some version of, "Good morning, Beautiful! Have an amazing day!"*

We all coped with the pandemic in our own way. On April 1st, Adam asked me the most random question.

Adam: If I invented a social media social distancing reality show, would you be interested in participating?

Me: As long as it's not challenges like *Survivor* <crying laughing emojis>

Adam: Welllll, it's going to be based on *Survivor*. But not like eating weird things or living in the wild. Much more civilized. Hahaha.

How could I say no to that?

Little did I know what I'd agreed to. Adam stayed true to his word and didn't make us eat spoonfuls of ants. But he did ask his most competitive friends to join the fun. I really got to know them as we accepted "Category Is" challenges, trying to best the other team with our individual videos. Every day when it was time to vote someone out, my heart raced, and my palms got sweaty. I even voted for myself a few times. Despite the nerves and pressure, I was grateful for the creative distraction during lockdown.

Over and over that spring, I readjusted my expectations for daily life. So many events were canceled or played out differently than I'd imagined. I'd been looking forward to April 6, 2020, for four months—the finalization of my second divorce. It was often still hard to believe that I'd been divorced twice.

I knew on the day we filed that I no longer wanted to be his wife. But . . . annoying mandatory state waiting period.

While I wrestled with a roller coaster of emotions that spring, I still wanted to celebrate the closing of that chapter in my life. The universe handed me that chance on Christmas Eve. Well, Lucy did. Her show, that I was excited to perform in, was scheduled to take place four days after my divorce was final.

Once again, fucking Miss Rona. Show canceled.

And the final divorce hearing? I joined a conference call with a judge, a clerk, and my almost ex-husband. So very weird. I wondered during the entire call, is this really happening? Would I be officially divorced at the end of this conversation? I had to be.

Life goes on.

Ten days later, I struggled to focus on a work call. I could only attend so many video meetings in one day.

The Social Isolation Survivor group chat dinged with a notification. *Did you hear the governor extended our stay-at-home order until May 26th?*

The announcement caught me off guard. I knew it was coming. I shouldn't have been surprised. But the words in black and white hit me hard. Tears sprung to my eyes. And they kept on coming. I texted my colleague Patty.

Me: I'm officially losing it. I read about the at home order being extended, and I can't stop crying.

Patty: Oh no!

Within a minute, the phone rang. Patty listened without judgment. She let me know it was okay to be struggling with everything. I will forever be so grateful to her, and my other friends like her.

The next morning, I stumbled onto an intriguing video on social media. I'd met Ashley at a pre-pandemic networking event in November. Total boss, I'd followed her immediately. I blinked and rubbed my eyes when her video popped into my feed. A month into a global pandemic, she wore a bold red gown and pearls. I listened with curiosity and admiration.

"Let me answer a couple of question for you. Yes, this is a dress. And yes, it has a cape. You know why? It's #formalFriday! We are fashionistas. And we have been on lockdown, and we have been in yoga pants too long. My dear friend Dana pointed out to me that that is unacceptable, and it's actually hurting the fashion industry we love so dearly. So, I challenge you to get in a fancy dress and show up to a conference call today, next Friday, and the Friday after that. The other six days let's toooootally be in sweatpants and yoga pants. But until then, fancy dresses for all!"

I needed to do this. I was trying to join the fashion industry, for crying out loud. The challenge gave me something to look forward to every week. On #formalfridays, I felt a little safer at home.

By week four, coworkers asked me on Thursday what I'd be wearing the next day. Maybe because I'd shown up to a few video calls in a ballgown. On week two, I stayed in the floor-length red sequin gown for our group fitness session. Let me tell you, form-fitting sequins do not breathe.

Maybe that day I wasn't being so "safe at home."

NAME THAT BRAND

Back in January, a mentor had encouraged me to apply for the Governor's Business Plan Contest. I did it on a whim. Weeks later, I advanced to round two. A month and a half went by, and I'd almost forgotten about the contest. I practically fell off my chair when I saw the subject line pop up in an email.

Congrats! You're on to Phase 3 in the BPC.

I gasped. Jaw officially dropped. Yet another sign to move forward. The day after I was legally done with my marriage, my business had advanced to the next round of a prestigious contest. A business that started in my brain while I cried on the daily about my husband. Funny how timing worked sometimes.

A week later to the day, a woman named Janel emailed me. To fulfill a requirement for her capstone course, she was tasked with writing a story highlighting my business plan. Sure, the story might not be seen by anyone other than her professor, but it might be posted on the Wisconsin Governor's Business Plan Contest website. Either way, exciting.

She asked me how I'd decided to start my business.

I shared the highlights—when I was diagnosed, my choice to have a double mastectomy, wearing prosthetics until I chose not to anymore, and my inspiration to create a clothing line.

She was kind and thoughtful and made sure she understood each part of my story. She also asked how many women didn't have reconstructive surgery.

I talked about how it was a growing trend, for a variety of reasons, and about body positivity. "More and more people are coming to terms with the idea that we are more than our external bodies. I realized that I am more than my breasts." Then I brought up the movie *Love, Simon*. After Simon is publicly outed, he says, "I'm supposed to be the one who decides when and where and how and who knows and how I get to say it."

Let me be clear. I didn't compare any part of my cancer journey to being outed, but I did relate to the feeling of wanting to tell my story my way and in my own time. My cancer journey, and every part of it, was mine. I owned that narrative. I refused to relinquish that power to clothing that didn't fit. Everyone has a story to tell. Or not tell, if they prefer it that way.

I struggled with naming my brand for quite some time. Every time I thought of a cool name, I typed it into a search bar, only to find it existed already. Daydreaming one afternoon, I remembered the first time I saw *Waitress* in New York City. After the final curtain, Sara Bareilles came out on stage. The audience screamed and cheered for a solid two minutes. I thought she might say hello and be on her way. Oh no, she'd proceeded to choose various people from the audience to sing a song from the show. One after another, people bounded up to the stage for this karaoke night on steroids. Each person shared the lengths they'd gone to in order to be there that night. A fourteen-year-old had belted out a soulful ballad. I'd been in awe. And Sara had nodded and encouraged her by saying, "You do you, Sweets."

You do you, Sweets embodied the feeling of my clothing line. You do what's right for you. You make the decision that is best for you. You tell your story. I finally had my name.

YDY, Sweets.

You. Do. You.

FIXED

After a week of zero communication with Patrick, he emailed me with a volunteer event-related question. I answered like I would anyone else. Completely, with kindness, and a little sarcasm.

Within minutes, I had another message in the chat box.

And here we were again. I clicked on his profile, curious what he had been up to. His most recent post was an extensive goal-setting plan for his life. As a friend, I was super happy for him. As a potential romantic interest, where was there room for me in his life? More than an "I'll reach out when I happen to be free"? That I didn't want. No, thank you.

I messaged Max.

Me: He's back. Ish.

Max: Sigh. I hate him, Jaimie.

Me: He is 100% a FRIEND. You want to go after all your life goals? Good for you. Go get it. You want me as anything more than a friend? There is absolutely no time in there for me.

Max: THERE IT IS. Case closed. Cracked. Solved.

Me: Now if he wants to talk WHEN I'M AVAILABLE and tell me how amazing I am . . . I'll listen.

Max: YOU DID IT. I'M SO PROUD.

Me: YOU HELPED ME GET THERE.

Max: You crossed the finish line yourself, queen <heart emojis>

To quote Ms. Pope one more time, "Now, you can dance with me, or you can get off my dance floor. I'm fine dancing alone."

A few minutes later, "Fix You" came on Pandora.

I laughed. I needed to be more careful which songs I gave the thumbs up.

Funny how I'd thought I needed someone else to fix me when, through everything I went through, I finally fixed myself. With the greatest queens guiding me as I righted my crown.

ACKNOWLEDGMENTS

I am humbled and overwhelmed thinking about all the people who helped make this book a reality.

Jess Rausch, thank you again for encouraging me to read *Untamed*. I wouldn't have finished this book without reading Glennon's powerful words first.

Jenni Freitag, I was such a jerk to you when you asked how my writing was going. Thank you for giving me grace and introducing me to my fabulous editor Lori Freeland.

Barbara Zabawa, thank you for reminding me how important it is to share my story.

I am forever grateful for my draft readers, who gave me the encouragement to keep going and made my book better. Thank you so much, Shannon Trafton, Carissa Dietzler, Amy Ketchum, Kim Eley, and Michelle Kimple.

In the middle of a pandemic, so many authors, business connections, and dear friends shared their time and wisdom with me. Thank you so very much, JuliAnne Murphy, Adam Braatz, Ryan Birdsall, Becky Branton-Griemann, Lisa Koenecke, Leslie Ferris Yerger, Laura Ingalls, Chariti Gent, Liz Vander Woude, Erin Clune, Lila Holley, Mary Helen Conroy, and Marci Greenberg Cox.

Pasha Marlowe, thank you for being your amazing and vulnerable self and introducing me to our publisher Lil Barcaski. Lil, thank you for pushing and guiding me to make this book the best it could be.

Susan Johansson, you amaze and inspire me daily. Thank you to Susan Elizabeth Photography for capturing me so vividly and beautifully. You knew my vision before I did.

Avery and John, thank you for tolerating my exhaustion and short temper as I edited. I love you both so much.

To my FIVE family and my inner circle, I don't want to imagine where I'd be without you in my life. Thank you from the very bottom of my heart. I love you.

To my readers, thank you for being a part of my journey. I hope you found something you needed in my words.

JAIMIE SHERLING is a joy seeker, drag ambassador, and the founder/designer of YDY, Sweets—a clothing line created for her sister breast cancer survivors. She lives in Wisconsin with her two kids. When she's not working at her day job or trying on piles of clothes at thrift stores, you can find her screaming YAASSSS surrounded by a bunch of queens.

CPSIA information can be obtained
at www.ICGtesting.com
Printed in the USA
BVHW031642230921
617409BV00006B/500